GW00644844

SHIBORI

a beginner's guide to creating
color & texture on fabric

SHIBORI

a beginner's guide to creating color & texture on fabric

Lynne Caldwell

LARK BOOKS

A Division of Sterling Publishing Co., Inc.
New York

DEVELOPMENT EDITORS
Paige Gilchrist
Jane LaFerla
Valerie Shrader

LINE EDITOR
Jean Campbell

ART DIRECTOR
Stacey Budge

COVER DESIGNER
Barbara Zaretsky

ASSOCIATE EDITORS
Susan Kieffer
Nathalie Mornu

ASSISTANT EDITOR
Rebecca Guthrie

ASSOCIATE ART DIRECTOR
Shannon Yokeley

ASSISTANT ART DIRECTOR
Lance Wille

ART PRODUCTION ASSISTANT
Jeff Hamilton

EDITORIAL ASSISTANCE
Dawn Dillingham
Delores Gosnell

PROOFREADER
Karen Levy

ILLUSTRATOR
Bernadette Wolfe

PHOTOGRAPHER
Stewart O'Shields

Library of Congress Cataloging-in-Publication Data

Caldwell, Lynne, b. 1965-
  Shibori : a beginner's guide to creating color & texture on fabric / Lynne
Caldwell.
      p. cm.
  Includes bibliographical references and index.
  ISBN 1-57990-659-1 (hardcover)
  1. Textile design. I. Title.
TS1475.C25 2006
746.6--dc22
                                          2006006722

10 9 8 7 6 5 4 3 2 1

First Edition

Published by Lark Books, A Division of
Sterling Publishing Co., Inc.
387 Park Avenue South, New York, N.Y. 10016

Text © 2006, Lynne Caldwell
Photography © 2006, Lark Books
Illustrations © 2006, Lark Books

Distributed in Canada by Sterling Publishing,
c/o Canadian Manda Group, 165 Dufferin Street
Toronto, Ontario, Canada M6K 3H6

Distributed in the United Kingdom by GMC Distribution Services,
Castle Place, 166 High Street, Lewes, East Sussex, England BN7 1XU

Distributed in Australia by Capricorn Link (Australia) Pty Ltd.,
P.O. Box 704, Windsor, NSW 2756 Australia

The written instructions, photographs, designs, patterns, and projects in
this volume are intended for the personal use of the reader and may be
reproduced for that purpose only. Any other use, especially commercial
use, is forbidden under law without written permission of the copyright
holder.

Every effort has been made to ensure that all the information in this book
is accurate. However, due to differing conditions, tools, and individual
skills, the publisher cannot be responsible for any injuries, losses, and
other damages that may result from the use of the information in this
book.

If you have questions or comments about this book, please contact:
Lark Books
67 Broadway
Asheville, NC 28801
(828) 253-0467

Manufactured in China

All rights reserved

ISBN 13: 978-1-57990-659-7
ISBN 10: 1-57990-659-1

For information about custom editions, special sales, premium and corporate purchases, please contact Sterling
Special Sales Department at 800-805-5489 or specialsales@sterlingpub.com.

Contents

Introduction

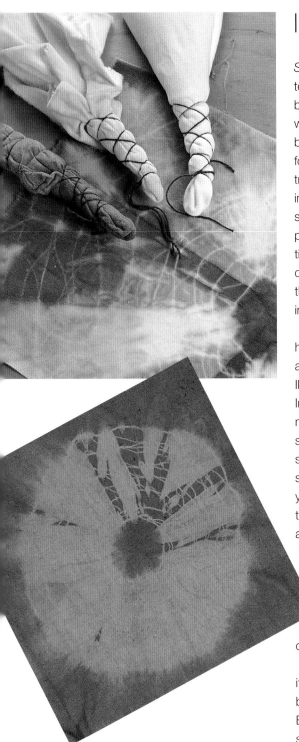

Shibori is the Japanese word for a technique in which fabric is shaped, bound, and dyed. We've adopted this word in the Western world to mean any bound, shaped-resist dyeing technique for cloth. It encompasses a variety of traditional methods of binding that include folding and clamping fabric into shape; stitching and gathering it; wrapping it around a pole; or binding it with ties. The fabric is then placed into a dye bath so that the bound portion of the fabric resists the dye and leaves interesting patterns and shapes.

My current fascination with shibori has evolved from an earlier interest in a resist-dyeing process known as *ikat*. Ikat is derived from the Malay-Indonesian word *mengikat,* which means to tie or to bind. (In fact, I was so taken with ikat that it was the subject of my master's thesis.) Unlike shibori, ikat involves tying and dyeing yarns *before* they are woven, rather than dyeing whole cloth—an intricate and time-consuming art form. The techniques used in shibori and ikat are similar, as are their histories.

But as my life became a bit more complicated (husband, children, and teaching), the relative simplicity of shibori began to appeal to me.

I think it's a perfect craft, because it not only has historical significance but also has varied levels of complexity. Even a novice can make exquisite shibori cloth, and because there's always more to learn, one doesn't tire of the technique. It requires a minimal amount of supplies, so it's inexpensive

to do and easy to get started. Shibori's accessibility makes it a great art form for anyone interested in fabric and fiber arts.

Cloth has been used for centuries to express family status, politics, emotion, and continuity. Because of its historical aspects and pure beauty, I find cloth and our relationship to it very compelling. We use cloth as part of ceremony and life rituals. The white of a bride's dress is symbolic of purity. Although this symbolism has faded in some respects, brides still wear white as a part of tradition. Family members often knit baby blankets for the newest members of their community. Graduates wear special gowns on graduation day. These cloths are often handed down as valued treasures that tie the past to the future. This has always been true of shibori, as the cloth has traditionally been used to mark life ceremonies, including wrapping a newborn baby as well as preparing the dead for burial. To begin working with this ancient technique is to bind yourself to the previous generations.

Historically, Japan is the country most well known for its exquisite shibori cloth, dating as far back as the eighth century. But there is evidence of early shibori textiles from all over the world, including Africa, India, Southeast Asia, and South America. More recently, the practice of tie-dye (which is actually a shibori technique called bound resist) became popular in the 1960s with the advance of cold-water dyes. The impact of that technique is still so strong that the mere mention of tie-dye evokes memories of that time in our history, with all its troubles and joys.

Though shibori is a time-honored medium of expression, it can—and should—be fun, too. I made some fascinating discoveries about color and design while I was working on this book, many of which surprised and delighted me. If you're prone to experimentation, shibori will be the perfect medium. In the pages that follow, I'll introduce you to four of the simplest methods of shibori, which are arashi (pole-wrapping), bound resists, stitching and gathering, and folding and clamping. For inspiration, you'll see a few projects completed from shibori cloth created from each technique, including those made from clothing "blanks" such as tees or scarves, and we'll also discuss adding embellishments to complement your shibori projects for a thoroughly modern look.

I invite you to join me in an exploration of shibori. Keep in mind its ancient traditions while you create contemporary designs, and I think you'll find personal meaning in the journey.

These historical examples of shibori are from different time periods.

Top: *Tunic, Pre-Columbian Peru, Middle Horizon, A.D. 600-900. Alpaca, plain weave, warps dovetailed over scaffold weft. Bound resist, reassembled in patchwork form. 4 x 6 feet (122 x 183 cm).*
© THE TEXTILE MUSEUM, WASHINGTON, D.C., 91.341

Right: *Suo sleeve fragment, Japanese, Edo period, 1st half 19th century. Plain weave ramie, resist dyed. 20⅛ x 12⅛ inches (51.2 x 30.7 cm).*
MUSEUM OF FINE ARTS, BOSTON; HARRIET OTIS CRUFT FUND, 28.491. PHOTOGRAPH © 2006 MUSEUM OF FINE ARTS, BOSTON

Getting Started

Let's begin to explore shibori by taking a quick overview of the process; then, in this first chapter, we'll discuss color, design, and fabric. Next, I'll show you how easy it is to set up a workspace, and we'll talk about the simple tools you need to get started. The second chapter is devoted to dyes and the various dyeing processes. Lastly, each of the four shibori methods in the book are described in chapters of their own.

*Arashi:
silk velvet
and acid dyes*

*Folding and
clamping: china
silk scarf and acid dye*

Shibori Methods

There are countless ways to make shibori fabric, but only four of the most simple methods are covered in this book: *arashi* (pole-wrapping), folding and clamping, bound resists, and stitching and gathering.

Arashi is a shibori method that involves wrapping fabric around a pole and then dipping the pole into a dye bath. This technique is amazingly flexible because you not only have the option to choose a planned or random pattern, but you can also finish the whole process—wrapping, dyeing, and rinsing the fabric—in less than 45 minutes.

Folding and clamping is another fast technique. You simply fold the fabric and bind it with a C-clamp or rubber band, and within minutes you're ready to drop the fabric into a dye bath.

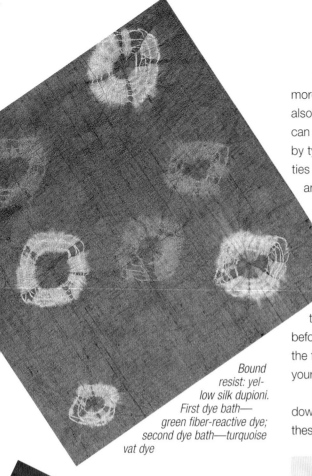

Bound resist: yellow silk dupioni. First dye bath—green fiber-reactive dye; second dye bath—turquoise vat dye

Bound resists may take a little more time to complete, but they're also accessible. In this process, you can make random or planned patterns by tying areas of fabric in place with ties (yarn, string, plastic, wire, etc.) and then placing them into the dye bath.

Stitching and gathering tends to be a more time-consuming process than the others but is still easy to do. Fabric is stitched and then gathered together and tied before dyeing. The resulting marks on the fabric are "drawn" according to your stitching.

Each process can be broken down into the simple steps shown on these pages.

1. Choosing a shibori process

Sttitching and gathering: silk charmeuse and acid dye

2. Manipulating the fabric into the desired design

3. Preparing a dye bath

Here's the finished piece of shibori cloth.

4. Dyeing the fabric

5. Rinsing the fabric

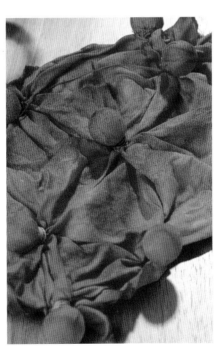

6. Allowing it to dry

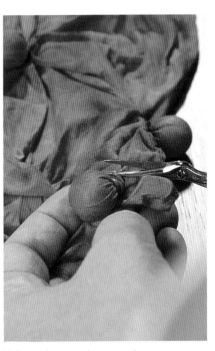

7. Removing any clamps or ties

Color and Ideas

Perhaps the first decision you'll make about your shibori project will involve color. Color can be an intimidating subject. Although you may know that red and blue make purple, what do scarlet and turquoise make? I think the best way to figure out color is to practice.

Sketching Ideas

First off, I like to make color sketches of what my shibori project might look like. If you feel daunted by this, don't— you shouldn't get too bogged down in the sketching process. If you're a

designer who works best flying by the seat of your pants, that's fine, too, but you may want to try making sketches for your first projects.

As I work my sketch to determine how the colors might go, I mentally walk through the dyeing process. For instance, if I decide to make a piece using blue and yellow dyes, I might take advantage of the fact that when blue and yellow dyes mix, they make green. So when I do my colored-pencil sketch, I'll include white, blue, yellow, and green areas. See the finished piece that I visualized on the next page.

Keeping a Dyer's Journal

An important step to successful dyeing is to set up a journal in which you can record your dye-mixing experiments. The book should list the way you mixed each batch of dye and include a dyed fabric swatch. It's smart to include mixes that weren't so successful, too. In the long run, the notebook will help you save lots of time (and even a little heartache) because you'll easily be able to review your previous experiments.

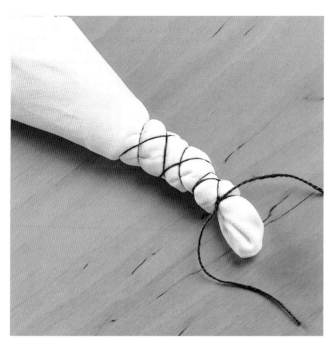

1. Begin with a white fabric and tie sections to resist the dye.

2. Dye the fabric yellow. Untie some of the white areas and tie over some of the yellow areas.

3. Dye the fabric blue.

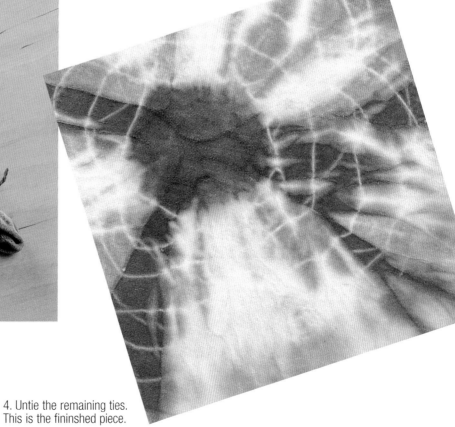

4. Untie the remaining ties. This is the fininshed piece.

13

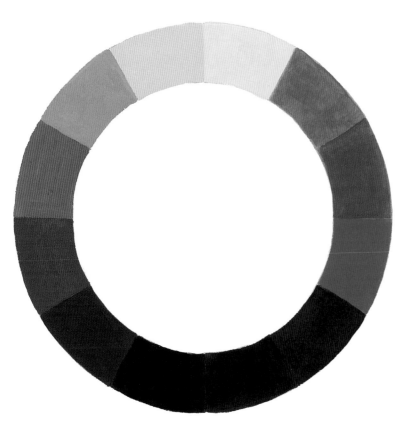

The color wheel

Experimenting with Dyes

I find that mixing and experimenting with dyes is half the fun when I make shibori cloth. If you aren't acquainted with dyes or dyeing, though, it's usually best to first research color swatches from fabric dye suppliers. You can buy these in the store, order them from the supplier, or often find them online. Then, when you're ready to buy dyes, you'll be armed with information about what's available.

There are many color choices, so to start out, I recommend sticking to primary colors (red, blue, and yellow) and buying two or three shades of each (for example, you might choose marigold, lemon, and straw in the yellow family).

Once you have these base colors to work with, you can mix them as you like to create brand-new colors. If this method of color mixing makes you nervous, just add a few secondary shades (purple, green, and orange) to your shopping basket.

Whichever way you go about it, the most important thing is to feel free to experiment and trust your color sense. Although you may not be a trained artist, you do know which colors you like, so just start by choosing colors you enjoy and think could work well together.

Once you've purchased your dye, follow the manufacturer's directions to mix a small batch. If you're directly mixing one dye with another to get a new color, take note of the ratios used to obtain the new color. For example, if you use ½ teaspoon (2.5 ml) of

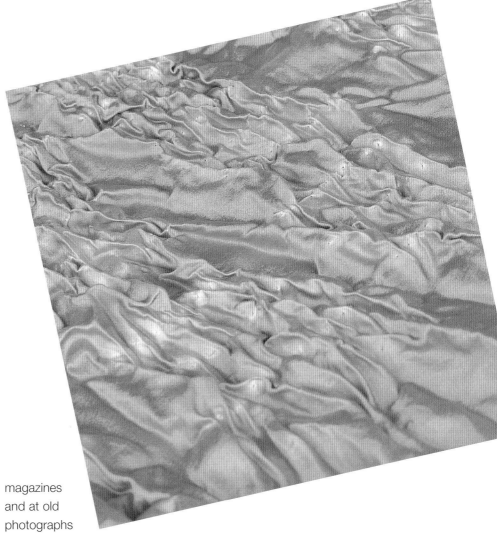

*Try using a primary color for
your first arashi pieces.*

crimson and ½ teaspoon (2.5 ml) of marigold, you have a 1:1 dye ratio. Once you've made up the dye, dip a small fabric swatch into the mix to see how you like the new color. If you like it, great! Start your larger shibori project using the dye ratio you used for your small swatch. If you don't like it, start over, but be sure to keep that first sample in your notebook for future reference.

Next, try a different approach by picking two colors that you like but think might not work together. See what happens.

If you're still uneasy about jumping in and experimenting with color, step back and look at the world around you. Pick rocks, leaves, and bark to create a color palette. Look in magazines and at old photographs for color combinations you like. This exercise may give you inspiration for your shibori color design. Inspiration can come from anywhere. For example, when I was in Maine a few years ago, I was struck by the way the sun hit underwater sea grass as I waded in Casco Bay. I had forgotten about the experience until one night during a birthing class. Our instructor taught us a visualization technique where we all closed our eyes and imagined walking down steps and opening a door into a peaceful, happy place. When I opened the door, I found myself back in Maine watching the sun on the sea grass. (On the way home from class I asked my husband where the door had opened for him and he answered, "Oakland Coliseum.")

The memory of the sun moving on that sea grass became a theme in my work for a long time. I tried very hard to capture in cloth the same feeling I had that day in Casco Bay. Of course, you can try to capture any place or feeling in your designs—even Oakland Coliseum.

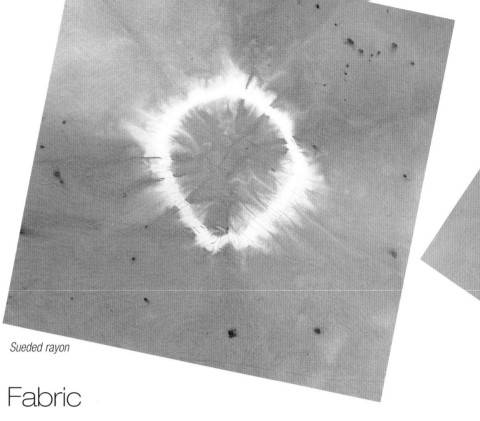

Sueded rayon

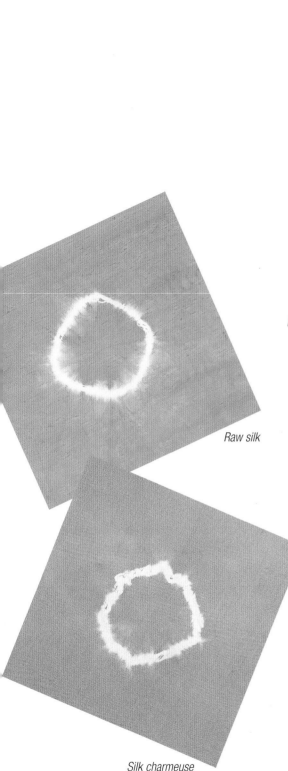

Raw silk

Silk charmeuse

Fabric

Anyone interested in this book is sure to be interested in fabric. Like most fiber lovers, I buy pieces of cloth just because they're beautiful, not because I have any real plan for them.

For your first shibori projects, I suggest buying a few yards of cotton sheeting and China silk. These two types of fabric are relatively inexpensive, and should free you up to experiment with dyes without worrying about making a costly mistake.

Once you've done a few color samples on the inexpensive stuff, you can go crazy with buying fabric. I like to go to upscale fabric shops that sell fine cottons and silks for wedding gowns. Keep in mind, however, that your base fabrics don't need to be bridal white. You can buy wonderful pre-dyed fabrics and dye directly over the existing color, you can undye (discharge—see page 32) the fabric, or both. I even use commercially pat-

terned material on occasion if it works well with a project I have in mind. I don't suggest spending a fortune on fantastic fabric and plunging it into a dye bath without first testing the colors on a small swatch, though. That said, some of my favorite pieces have been "happy accidents."

You can also buy ready-made clothing, accessories, draperies, and other finished textile pieces to create your shibori projects. The only drawback I see in using these is that the pressure to succeed is pretty high— you just have one shot at making a masterpiece. I usually work best without that kind of pressure, but if you feel certain of the technique and dyes you're using, there's no reason why a ready-made piece won't work for you. I find that using stained or accidentally bleached clothing works well because a lot of that pressure to succeed is off my shoulders. If I don't like the results,

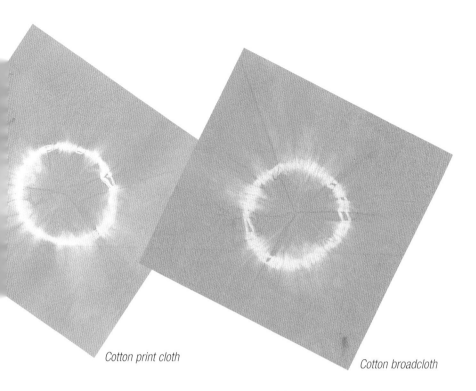

Cotton print cloth

Cotton broadcloth

Fabric Types

There are many kinds of dyes and fabrics, and only a few are addressed in this book. While it's possible to dye synthetic fibers at home or in your studio, I've chosen to focus on natural fibers because the options for dyeing them are greater.

Cellulose fibers, which are referred to in the dyeing section, are fibers that come from plants and share a common molecular structure. Cotton, linen, rayon, and hemp fall into this category. Protein fibers, such as silk and wool, are animal rather than plant fibers. Each fabric has its own feel when you're manipulating it. After you choose the appropriate fabric, you'll need to decide which dye will work best with it.

it's not a problem. And for those successes, it's amazing how shibori can reinvigorate your closet.

No matter what fabric you use, you'll need to scour it (page 24) before you begin your project. Scouring removes sizing (a mixture sometimes added to fabric to stiffen it) and enables the fabric to hold the dye better. I actually scour any fabric I'm using before starting a project, even if it hasn't been treated with sizing. I find it allows the fabric to dye more evenly.

One of the fascinating things about experimenting with fabric and dye is discovering how the various fabrics respond to the dyeing process. (I have my favorites, and you'll probably find yours, too.) In the series of photos on these pages, note the different outcomes when various fabrics were dyed in the same dye bath, using the bound resist technique. Refer to these photos to see the difference that the fabric can make.

Making a Fabric Notebook

Although it's not required to get started on your shibori project, I recommend keeping a collection of fabric swatches. Add velvet, organza, chenille, rayon, etc. to your collection so you can get a feel for which ones you like best. Label each swatch so you know what to ask for in case you'd like to buy that fabric again.

Next, create small shibori pieces with the swatches so you know how the dye takes to the fabric and which shibori technique works best. Keep the color samples in a notebook, and you'll find yourself referring to them again and again.

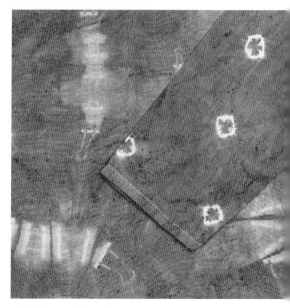

This blouse had a stubborn stain, so I used it as a canvas for experimenting with design and color.

You don't need a large workspace to create shibori.

Setting Up Your Workspace

There are basically two steps to making shibori cloth: creating the resist (tying, wrapping, and/or binding the fabric) and dyeing the fabric. Most of the work, however, is done in that first stage before the dyes are even brought out. Because this stage is often long and involved, I find I move my project from one part of my house to another so I can tie or wrap as I wish. And if I'm working on a random pattern using a binding technique, the cloth and ties often go with me wherever I go—even in the car, if someone else is driving.

For years I dreamed of having my own dyeing studio where I could dye my shibori fabric in a freestanding sink. It's been great to have that space, mostly because I now can leave my mess and come back to it later, but I don't think it's made any difference in my designs—like I mentioned earlier, most of the work in shibori is done in that first stage.

To set yourself up for basic dyeing, you really just need to have a source of running water, a sturdy table, and, if you're using a type of dye that needs heat, some type of burner. Although it seems to make sense to do this all in the kitchen, it isn't the best place to work with dyes because none of the chemicals used with dyeing should be ingested. Keep that in mind, too, when choosing utensils to stir solutions and dye baths—if you use food utensils for dyeing, don't reuse them for food preparation.

So, a bathroom, garage, laundry room, and outdoors are all good options for a dyeing workspace. In any of these places you'll need to have a table on which you can set all your dyeing supplies. I wouldn't suggest using an expensive wooden table for your projects. Wood is a fiber and you'll probably be working with fiber-reactive dyes, meaning that your nice table could be permanently stained. I find that inexpensive laminate-topped folding tables work well. They are easy to clean and can be quickly taken down when you're done. Another option is to make a table using sawhorses and a piece of plywood. If you don't want dye to seep into the plywood, just cover it with plastic sheeting or even garbage bags.

Another consideration for your dyeing space is the floor. The best-case scenario is a floor that doesn't need to be clean or stain-free, such as in a garage. But if your space has tile flooring and you don't want dye in the

Workspace Safety

Fabric dyes and the other supplies used in dyeing (auxiliaries) are completely safe to work with as long as you use them properly. There are, however, several important safety considerations no matter which kind of dye you use or where you plan to dye.

- Don't eat, drink, or smoke in an area where dyes and chemicals are used.

- Don't ever breathe in dye powder, and take every precaution not to spill the powder. If you do spill it, wipe it up immediately with a wet sponge. When working with the powder you should use a well-fitting dust mask that you can pick up from any hardware store. Respirators are also great and especially necessary when discharging fabric because of the fumes. You can buy cartridges for your respirator that are made for working with dust and fumes.

- Always wear gloves. Although it may look fun to walk around with blue or orange hands, it's not good for you. Just know that it's a good idea to keep the dye on the fabric and not on or in you.

- Good ventilation is very important. Only mix dye in an area that is constantly circulating fresh air. But don't use a fan near chemicals and never mix powders near furnace or air-conditioner intake pipes.

- Don't sweep floors and surfaces. Vacuum them instead.

- Wear goggles when working with corrosive materials such as acetic acid.

- Keep dyes and auxiliaries in safe storage away from children and pets.

- Don't dispose of dye waste in the ground—the sewer system is designed to handle these wastes. But concentrated highly acidic or alkaline wastewater can upset the balance of a septic system. If you have questions about disposal, contact your local board of health for guidelines specific to your area.

You can get a materials safety data sheet on any dyeing product from the supplier to find out chemical details and safety issues. These sheets detail precautions and potential health hazards on dye products.

grout, cover the floor with plastic sheeting. The same goes with a carpeted workspace.

You'll also need a place to hang your dyed fabric to dry, and an outdoor clothesline or garage work well because you don't need to worry about any possible dye drips. In the days before my studio, I hung fabric on the shower rod in my bathroom, and that works fine, too. Just be sure to cover the area where the fabric may drip.

If you'll be working in a place other than a studio or craft room, consider designating a laundry basket and some plastic containers just for your shibori projects. This can serve as your traveling studio, keeping all your dyeing supplies and other tools in one place. Once you have all of these materials organized and on hand, you'll find that your setup and takedown time will only be about 5 to 10 minutes.

Tools and Supplies

Many of the items you'll use for projects in this book are probably lying around your house at the moment. I know I can usually find something I need in my kitchen junk drawer.

BURNER. A small burner is used to heat an acid or vat dye bath.

CHALK OR WATER-SOLUBLE CRAYON. There are a few projects in this book where you'll need to draw directly onto the fabric. I recommend using chalk or water-soluble crayon for these projects because pencil doesn't always wash out of fabric.

CLAMPS. You'll need C-clamps, as well as other types of clamps such as spring clamps and binder clips, for the folding and clamping method. Rubber bands also work for securing fabric, but do so with less rigidity than C-clamps and leave extra marks on the fabric.

CLOTHESLINE OR DRYING RACK. This is essential for hanging fabrics after they've been dyed and rinsed.

COOKING POT. Use a large, non-corrosive cooking pot for acid or vat dyeing.

DUST MASK OR RESPIRATOR. Use a dust mask or respirator to protect yourself from breathing in dye powder or other dry auxiliaries (the additional supplies needed for the dyeing process).

IRON. I have several irons in my studio. I suggest that you relegate one iron for working with undyed fabric and another for dyed fabrics. If you use the same iron, you'll find that sometimes a bit of dye remains on the cloth and could inadvertently be transferred to the iron and then to another piece of clean cloth. If you don't want to invest in more than one iron, just make sure that you clean it after each use on dyed fabric.

LAUNDRY BASKET. I use a laundry basket to store my supplies so that I can easily move a project around with me.

MASKING TAPE. This is a very useful tool because it helps you steady the fabric when you begin a project.

MEASURING CUP. A 2-cup (.5 l) glass measuring cup is perfect to measure supplies like salt, but I also find it excellent for mixing dyes and other chemicals. Rarely will you need anything larger than 2 cups (.5 l). The handle and spout are very easy to work with.

MEASURING SPOONS. These are for measuring small amounts of dye and other chemicals.

PENCILS AND PAPER. I begin almost every project with a lead pencil and paper to sketch out my fabric pattern design. I then fill in my sketches with colored pencils.

PLASTIC BUCKET. You'll need at least one large plastic bucket for dyeing with cold-water dyes.

PLASTIC CUPS WITH LIDS OR MASON JARS. These containers are great for storing stock solutions.

PLASTIC OR WOOD SHAPES. For folding and clamping, you'll need two pieces of plastic or wood of the same shape. For example, if you're designing a piece of cloth with triangles, the fabric should fit between two triangle shapes.

PLASTIC SHEETING. This is used to cover the area beneath your dye space, protecting it from spills.

PLASTIC SPOONS. Large plastic mixing spoons come in handy when stirring dye baths (just don't use them in the kitchen once they've been used for dyeing). Small, disposable plastic spoons are handy for mixing dye powder into paste and making stock solutions. It's easiest to mix several colors at a time without having to clean the spoon completely between each color.

PVC PIPE. This very strong plastic piping is inexpensive, and, best of all, won't absorb dye. It's perfect for making arashi fabric—when I wrap fabric around PVC pipe and then pull the ties around it over and over again, I never worry about breaking the pipe. You can find PVC pipe in the plumbing

section of any hardware store. I suggest getting 3-foot (.9 m) lengths of it in two different diameters. You may want to get longer pieces, but consider the fact that your pipe needs to be only a little longer than the depth of the bucket you're dyeing the fabric in.

QUILTING THREAD. You'll need thread to work the stitching and gathering method, and quilting thread is very strong. Using a bright color can help you see your design as you work.

SCALE. You'll need to use a scale only if you plan on re-creating colors precisely or dyeing large amounts of fabric. I like to see what happens with color and allow my projects to change as I go, so I rarely work with exact weights.

SCISSORS. I carry a small pair of scissors with me almost everywhere I go.

Although you may want a large pair of scissors for cutting fabric, you'll find that small, sharp, pointed embroidery scissors are invaluable when it comes to cutting very small threads that have been tightly gathered around a fine piece of cloth.

SEWING NEEDLES. You'll need sewing needles in varying sizes for the stitching and gathering method. You'll use a small, sharp needle when working with thin fabrics such as China silk, and large needles for a medium-to-heavyweight fabric such as cotton broadcloth.

SPONGES AND RAGS. Have plenty of sponges and rags on hand to clean up spills.

THERMOMETER. A studio thermometer is necessary so you can check the heat of your acid or vat dye baths.

TIES. It's great to have a variety of tying materials to create the varying patterns in your projects. I like to use different sizes of yarn, string, plastic, rug warp, and wire. The ties you choose for securing your shibori projects before you dye them can make a huge difference in the outcome of your design. I like to use 3/2 perle cotton or even rug warp. They both leave very fine lines on the finished piece and are easy to handle. They are also strong. When pulled tightly, they are excellent in resisting dye. When I want to make thick lines, I use strips of strong plastic. You can make them by cutting up garbage bags or using ikat tape (a very strong plastic). Thick rubber bands also work well.

MISCELLANEOUS OBJECTS. For the chapter on bound resists, I recommend gathering various objects from around the house, including unpopped popcorn, coins, and bottle caps. You'll wrap cloth around these and then tie the fabric to capture them within. Unpopped popcorn will give you a very small circular design, while coins make larger circular designs. Bottle caps can be stuffed with fabric and then tied to make a funky circular design. (When you get to this section, don't substitute dried beans for popcorn! I did this once on China silk, and after leaving it to soak overnight, I found in the morning that the beans had expanded—as beans will do in water—and the cloth was torn.)

Dyes and Recipes

While the patterns and shapes you create from the resists define shibori, dyeing is a major part of the process. In this chapter, we'll explore the methods I used to create the samples you see in *Shibori*, but first, a quick word about the additional supplies you'll need to dye your shibori cloth.

Supplies

ACETIC ACID. Works like vinegar but is eleven times stronger.

ALBEGAL SET. Used with acid dyes to achieve even colors.

ANTI-CHLOR CONCENTRATE. Neutralizes chlorine after removing color from fabric.

BLEACH. Used to remove color from fabric.

CITRIC ACID CRYSTALS. May be interchanged with acetic acid or vinegar.

DYE ACTIVATOR OR SODA ASH (SODIUM CARBONATE). Raises the pH of the dye bath and fixes the dye to the fabric.

LYE (SODIUM HYDROXIDE). A strong alkali used with vat dyes and indigo, lye helps prepare certain dye baths for the reduction process.

METAPHOS (SODIUM HEXAMETAPHOS-PHATE). A water softener. If using hard water, it improves the absorption of dye.

NON-IODIZED SALT. Creates an electro-static charge in the dye bath that forces color into the cloth.

SODIUM ACETATE CRYSTALS. An acid-forming salt that works with acid dyes to achieve even colors.

THIOX (THIOUREA DIOXIDE). Used to strip color from cellulose and protein fibers.

WHITE DISTILLED VINEGAR. Lowers the pH of the dye bath and helps fix the dye to the fabric.

Dyeing Methods

There are many different recipes for working with dyes for shibori. The following information can be used as a guide for dyeing fabric, but you should always follow the manufacturer's directions. When you buy dye and auxiliaries (the items listed above) from any supplier, be sure to ask for specific dyeing instructions. Refer to the Dyeing Terms at the right as needed.

In a few instances, you'll see identical amounts of supplies listed to produce two different shades (i.e., light and medium). To create a darker shade, simply leave the fabric in the dye bath for a longer amount of time.

NOTE

All the dye recipes are meant for 1 pound (.45 kg) of dry fabric unless otherwise stated.

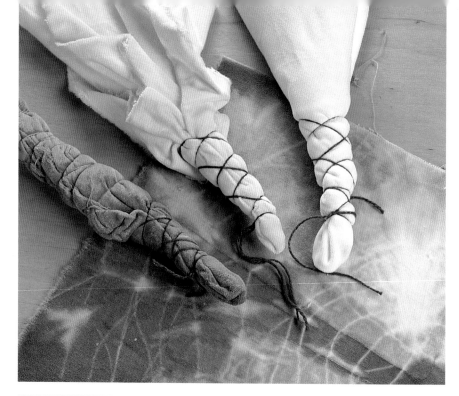

Dyeing Terms

Discharge. Removing color from fabric.

Dye bath. Used in this book to refer to immersion dyeing of fabric.

Immersion dyeing. Submerging fabric in a dye bath.

Over-dyeing. Dyeing a fabric more than once.

Oxidization. Chemical reaction that occurs when a fabric dyed with indigo or vat dyes is removed from its low-oxygen or "leuco" environment and exposed to air. Oxidization fixes the dye to the fabric. See also *reducing*.

Pasting out. The process of adding small amounts of water to dye and slowly stirring to remove lumps until the dye is smooth and will disperse easily in a bucket of water.

Reducing. The act of removing oxygen from a dye bath. Dyes that aren't soluble in water must be reduced with various chemical agents.

Scouring. Removing any excess fabric sizing that could inhibit the dye from taking hold. To scour, simply machine wash your fabric in hot water with ½ teaspoon (2.5 ml) of laundry detergent and ½ teaspoon (2.5 ml) of soda ash per pound of fabric. Rinse thoroughly.

Stock solution. A mixture of water and dye without an activating agent.

Vat dye. A particular type of dye that is very much like indigo. It is explained in depth on page 31.

Fiber-Reactive Dyes

Fiber-reactive dyes are particularly formulated to work on cotton, silk, linen, and rayon fabrics. They are colorfast, washfast, and lightfast and actually create a chemical bond with the fiber. This type of dye is so good at what it does that it often seeps right through an area of resist. So, if you choose to use a fiber-reactive dye, tie each resist very tightly or expect the colors to bleed into one another. You can use this property to your advantage if this is the effect you seek.

The availability range of fiber-reactive dye colors is extraordinary. But remember—mixing your own dye colors is half the fun, so don't buy too many colors when getting started.

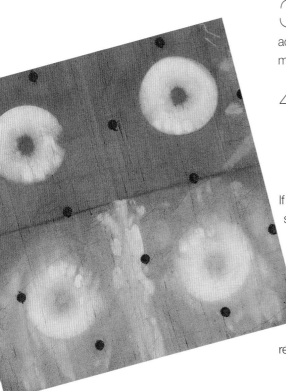

Immersion Dyeing with Fiber-Reactive Dyes

What You Do

1 Scour the fabric with laundry detergent and soda ash. Let it dry and create the resists. Set aside.

2 Wearing rubber gloves, paste out the dye powder in a measuring cup by slowly adding 1 cup (.25 l) of water to the dye and stirring with a plastic spoon. Use measuring spoons and the chart below to determine how much dye to use for your desired shade. Set the pasted-out solution aside.

> **LIGHT:** 1 teaspoon (5 ml)
> **MEDIUM:** 3 teaspoons (15 ml)
> **DARK:** 6 teaspoons (30 ml)

3 Fill the large bucket with 2½ gallons (9.5 l) of cool water. Once added, the fabric should be able to move freely in the water.

4 Add salt to the water according to your desired shade.

> **LIGHT:** 1 pound (.45 kg)
> **MEDIUM:** 1½ pounds (.68 kg)
> **DARK:** 2 pounds (.9 kg)

If desired, add Metaphos in the amount suggested by the manufacturer.

5 Add the pasted-out dye to the saltwater and stir. Dampen the fabric and add it to the bath. To get even results, stir continuously for 10 to 15 minutes; to get mottled results, do not stir. Set aside.

6 Dissolve the dye activator or soda ash in another measuring cup by slowly making a paste with 2 cups (.5 l) of warm water. Use the amount indicated for your desired shade. Set aside.

> **LIGHT:** 5 tablespoons (75 ml)
> **MEDIUM:** 5 tablespoons (75 ml)
> **DARK:** 7 tablespoons (105 ml)

What You Need

Laundry detergent

Soda ash

Ties and other resists

Rubber gloves

1 to 6 teaspoons (5 to 30 ml) fiber-reactive dye powder

2 medium glass or plastic measuring cups

Several gallons (liters) water

Plastic spoon

Measuring spoons

1 large plastic, stainless steel, enamel, or nonreactive metal bucket

1 to 2 pounds (.5 to 1 kg) non-iodized salt

5 to 7 tablespoons (75 to 105 ml) dye activator or soda ash

Scale (optional)

Metaphos (optional)

7 Wearing rubber gloves, take the fabric out of the dye bath and pour in the dissolved activator or soda ash. Stir the dye and put the fabric back into the bucket. Stir continuously for the first 5 minutes, then stir every 5 minutes for the next 60 minutes to get even results. Stir less often to achieve mottled results.

8 Remove the fabric from the dye bath and pour the dye down the drain. Rinse the fabric thoroughly in a bucket of room-temperature water, changing the water several times until the water is clear. Hang to dry.

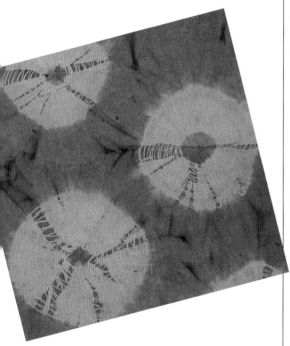

Immersion Dyeing with Fiber-Reactive Dyes in the Washing Machine

Amounts are for 8 pounds (3.6 kg) of dry fabric. Adjust amounts accordingly.

What You Do

1 Scour the fabric with laundry detergent and soda ash. Let it dry and create the resists. Set aside.

2 Wearing rubber gloves, paste out the dye powder in a measuring cup by slowly adding 1 cup (.25 l) of water to the dye and stirring with a plastic spoon. Use measuring spoons and the chart below to determine how much dye to use for your desired shade. Set the pasted-out solution aside.

> **LIGHT:** 5 teaspoons (25 ml)
> **MEDIUM:** 5 tablespoons (75 ml)
> **DARK:** 10 tablespoons (150 ml)

3 Set the washing machine for a large load and a warm water setting. Once the machine is full of water and begins agitating, add the salt according to the shade you desire and let the machine agitate until all of the salt is dissolved.

> **LIGHT:** 5 pounds (2.3 kg)
> **MEDIUM:** 7½ pounds (3.4 kg)
> **DARK:** 10 pounds (4.5 kg)

If desired, add Metaphos in the amount suggested by the manufacturer.

What You Need

- Laundry detergent
- Soda ash
- Ties and other resists
- Rubber gloves
- 5 teaspoons (25 ml) to 10 tablespoons (150 ml) fiber-reactive dye powder
- 2 medium glass or plastic measuring cups
- Several gallons (liters) water
- Plastic spoon
- Measuring spoons
- 5 to 10 pounds (2.3 to 4.5 kg) non-iodized salt
- ¾ to 2¼ cups (.2 to .5 l) dye activator or soda ash
- Scale (optional)
- Metaphos (optional)

4 Add the pasted-out dye to the agitating machine. Dampen the fabric and then put it evenly into the machine. Let the machine run for approximately 15 minutes, making sure that you don't let the dye go down the drain.

5 Dissolve the dye activator or soda ash slowly, making a paste with 2 cups (.5 l) of warm water. Use the amount indicated for your desired shade. Set aside.

LIGHT: ¾ cup (.2 l)
MEDIUM: 1½ cups (.4 l)
DARK: 2¼ cups (.5 l)

6 Wearing rubber gloves, move the fabric to one side of the machine and pour in the dissolved activator or soda ash. Stir and redistribute fabric. Allow the machine to agitate for 5 minutes and let it rest for 5 minutes; repeat for 60 minutes. Allow the machine to complete its cycle.

7 Reset the machine for a hot wash and warm rinse, add laundry detergent, and run a complete cycle. After the final spin, remove the fabric and hang to dry.

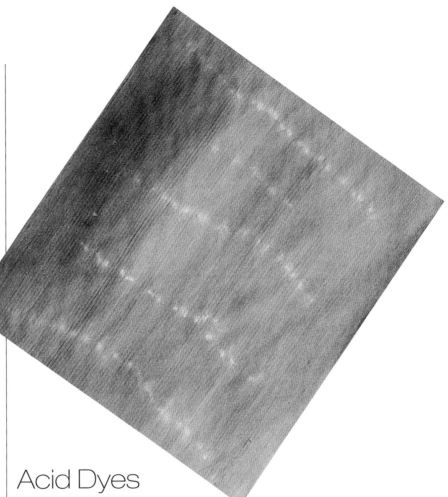

Acid Dyes

Acid dyes are an excellent choice when working on silk, wool, and nylon. The colors are incredibly rich and permanent. There are a couple of reasons why these dyes are so wonderful to work with when creating shibori pieces. First, when fabric is put into the dye bath, the dye won't seep through a resist, so the markings are stronger than they tend to be with fiber-reactive dyes. Also, the dye in these baths, when mixed in the exact proportion to the weight of the fabric, will become completely absorbed into the fabric, leaving the bath exhausted of dye. After dyeing you will end up with what may look like a clear bucket of water because all the dye goes into the fabric. Plus, rinsing the fabric will not change the color significantly. Unlike fiber-reactive dyes, which lighten several shades as the cloth dries, acid dyes give a truer indication of the final color, even when the fabric is wet.

The drawback to working with acid dyes is that there are more chemicals and more steps to the process, including heating the dye bath at a very slow rate. Depending on your workspace, this can be a little more challenging, but it's certainly not impossible.

Immersion Dyeing with Acid Dyes

What You Do

1 Scour the fabric with laundry detergent and soda ash. Let it dry and create the resists. Set aside.

2 Wearing rubber gloves and using the measuring spoons, measure the amount of dye for your desired shade into the 2-cup (.5 l) container.

  LIGHT: ½ teaspoon (2.5 ml)
  MEDIUM: 1¾ teaspoons (8.8 ml)
  DARK: 3½ teaspoons (17.5 ml)

3 Dissolve the dye by adding 1 cup (.2 l) of boiling water for light and medium shades and 2 cups (.5 l) of boiling water for dark shades. Stir thoroughly with a spoon and set aside to cool while making the dye bath.

4 Pour 3½ gallons (13.2 l) of room-temperature water into a stainless steel pot. The pot should be large enough to allow the fiber to move freely without spilling the dye bath. Add the items listed in the following order, stirring thoroughly after the addition of each one.

  DISSOLVED DYE
  CITRIC ACID CRYSTALS OR VINEGAR
  SODIUM ACETATE CRYSTALS
  SALT
  ALBEGAL SET

5 Dampen the fabric, add it to the dye bath, and stir. Place the pot on the burner and gradually—over a period of 30 to 40 minutes—raise the temperature to a boil, stirring the bath intermittently. If you are dyeing silk, only raise the temperature to a simmer—180°F (82°C).

6 Allow the dye bath to cool to room temperature. Remove the fabric and rinse well in warm water until the water runs clear. Squeeze out the excess water and hang to dry.

What You Need

- Laundry detergent
- Soda ash
- Rubber gloves
- Measuring spoons
- ½ to 3½ teaspoons (2.5 to 17.5 ml) acid dye powder
- 2-cup glass or plastic measuring cup
- Burner (for heating water)
- Several gallons (liters) of water
- Plastic spoon
- Large stainless steel pot
- 1 tablespoon (15 ml) citric acid crystals or 11 tablespoons (165 ml) white distilled vinegar
- 4 teaspoons (20 ml) sodium acetate crystals
- 5 teaspoons (25 ml) non-iodized salt
- 1 teaspoon (5 ml) Albegal SET
- Thermometer

Indigo

Indigo is a blue dye originally made from the tropical indigo plant, but is now available in a synthetic form. It is a traditional dye for shibori cloth, and has been used around the world to create fascinating effects. One piece of cloth can be dyed over and over again, creating a terrific value scale of blues. The resulting dyed fabric is extremely colorfast.

A fascinating part of the indigo process is watching the dye oxidize as it comes out of the dye bath and hits the air. Indigo is only soluble in its reduced, or oxygen-free, form. The color literally changes before your eyes, and there's no stopping it—the oxidization will continue until the cloth is blue.

Creating an indigo bath is a two-step process: making the stock solution and preparing the bath. Although it's a bit more complicated than the previous dye recipes, the results are fantastic.

Indigo is different from other dyes in that it is not water-soluble, i.e., the dye doesn't dissolve in water. Because of this property, the dye must be reduced by having oxygen removed through the addition of additional chemicals. These chemicals—such as lye—are very caustic, so this dyeing process should include extra care.

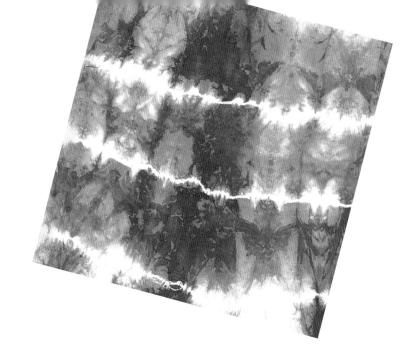

Immersion Dyeing with Indigo on Cotton, Linen, Rayon, and Silk

The following is based on a 4-gallon (15.2 l) dye bath, not on the weight of the fabric. The amount of fabric used in this recipe must fit into a 4-gallon (15.2 l) dye bath.

What You Do

1 Scour the fabric with laundry detergent and soda ash. Let it dry and create the resists. Set aside.

2 Put on the rubber gloves. In one of the measuring cups, combine the indigo powder with enough lukewarm water to make a lump-free paste. Stir with a spoon and set aside.

3 Measure 1½ cups (.3 l) of cold water into the second measuring cup. Add the lye, stir, and set aside to cool.

4 In the third measuring cup, combine 1 teaspoon (5 ml) of the Thiox with ½ cup (.1 l) of warm water and stir. Set aside.

What You Need

Laundry detergent

Soda ash

Rubber gloves

4 glass or plastic measuring cups

3 tablespoons (45 ml) synthetic indigo powder

Several gallons (liters) water

Plastic spoon

5 teaspoons (25 ml) lye (sodium hydroxide)

1½ teaspoons (7.5 ml) Thiox (thiourea dioxide)

1 large plastic, stainless steel, enamel, or nonreactive metal bucket

1 teaspoon (5 ml) Metaphos

¼ cup (.06 l) non-iodized salt

2 tablespoons (30 ml) distilled white vinegar (for silk)

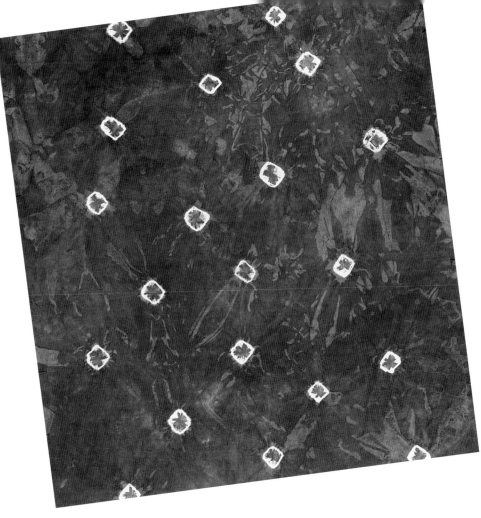

30 to 60 minutes. It's possible for this step to take up to 6 hours.

12 Wearing rubber gloves, dampen the fabric. Push the scum aside before lowering the fabric into the dye bath. Keep in mind that the places where the scum adheres to the cloth will end up lighter than the rest of the cloth (it will be acting as a resist).

13 Very gently and without splashing, submerge the fabric into the vat. Maneuver the cloth, always working below the surface of the bath, so the dye can completely penetrate the fabric. Submerge the fabric for 2 to 3 minutes.

14 Squeeze out any excess dye beneath the surface of the dye bath and then pull the fabric out. Don't let any dye drip back into the bath.

15 Let the fabric oxidize (it will turn blue) for approximately 15 minutes. You may repeat the dipping and oxidizing process until you've reached the shade of blue you like. Keep in mind that the final blue will be one or two shades lighter than when the fabric is wet.

16 For cotton and rayon, wash the fabric in hot water for 10 minutes with a capful of detergent. Stir the wash bath occasionally and rinse the fabric until the water runs clear. Hang to dry.

17 If you're dyeing silk, make an acid soak to help set the color by mixing the vinegar in 1 gallon (3.8 l) of room-temperature water. Let the fabric soak for 10 minutes, then rinse thoroughly with plain water.

5 Slowly add the lye solution to the pasted-out indigo and stir until smooth.

6 Add the Thiox solution and stir. Try not to add bubbles into the mix. This is your stock solution.

7 Stir the stock solution gently from time to time, until the mixture turns yellow. This indicates that the solution is reduced. If the solution is not properly reduced, the surface of the solution turns a deep blue from oxygen coming into contact with the dye. Reduction should be complete in less than an hour. Set the stock solution aside.

8 Fill the large bucket with 3 gallons (11.4 l) of water. Add the Metaphos and salt.

9 Use the fourth measuring cup to dissolve the remaining ½ teaspoon (2.5 ml) of Thiox in a small amount of warm water. Add it to the dye bath.

10 Add the stock solution to the dye vat by carefully lowering the container into the vat and pouring the liquid out at an angle. Stir gently.

11 After 30 to 60 minutes the dye bath should be a clear greenish-yellow with a shiny, dark blue metallic surface scum. If the bath is not clear and greenish-yellow, wait an additional

Vat Dyes

Vat dyes are similar to indigo in that they are not soluble in water. The dyes must be reduced to take to cellulose or silk fibers. Reduction takes place between 120° and 140°F (43° and 56°C). The dye turns a completely different color when it is reduced and will only return to its true color when it has been oxidized.

Vat dyes are particularly interesting for use with shibori because they can at once remove dye from fabric and replace it with another color. It is one of the most magical dyeing experiences ever! In other words, you may tie a resist on a green piece of fabric and then dye the fabric purple in a vat dye. When you are done, the resulting dyed area will not look like mud as you might expect. Instead, you will have a fabric dyed purple with green areas that were tied up. It's fantastic.

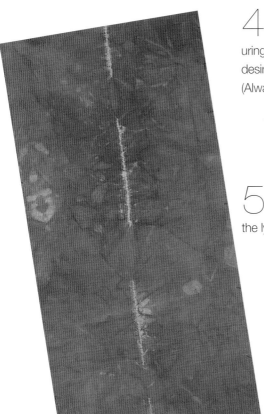

Immersion Dyeing with Vat Dyes

What You Do

1 Scour the fabric with laundry detergent and soda ash. Let it dry and create the resists. Set aside.

2 Measure 2½ gallons (9.5 l) of lukewarm water into the pot. The container should be large enough for the fabric to move freely without spilling.

3 Wearing rubber gloves, use measuring spoons and the chart below to measure the desired amount of dye powder in 1 cup (.2 l) of room-temperature water, stir with a plastic spoon, and set aside. If you are going for a light or medium shade, still use the amounts listed for dark below, but remove the fabric after a minimum of 2 minutes in the dye bath.

> **DARK:** 3 tablespoons (45 ml)
> **BLACK:** 6 tablespoons (90 ml)

4 Measure 1 cup (.2 l) of cold water and pour it into the second measuring cup. Carefully add the lye in the desired amount, using the chart below. (Always add lye to *cold* water!)

> **ALL SHADES EXCEPT BLACK:**
> 2 tablespoons (30 ml)
> **BLACK:** 4 tablespoons (60 ml)

5 Measure the Thiox according to the chart below and dissolve it in the lye solution.

> **ALL SHADES EXCEPT BLACK:**
> 2½ teaspoons (12.5 ml)
> **BLACK:** 5 teaspoons (25 ml)

What You Need

- Laundry detergent
- Soda ash
- Several gallons (liters) water
- 1 large stainless steel pot
- Rubber gloves
- Measuring spoons
- Plastic spoon
- 3 tablespoons (45 ml) vat dye powder
- 2 glass measuring cups
- Plastic spoons
- 2 to 6 tablespoons (30 to 60 ml) lye (sodium hydroxide)
- 2½ to 5 teaspoons (12.5 to 25 ml) Thiox (thiourea dioxide)
- Burner
- Thermometer

6 Stir the dissolved dye, lye, and Thiox into the dye bath water, put the pot on the burner, and heat to 140°F (56°C). Once the bath reaches this temperature, it should be fully reduced. You can tell when the bath has been reduced by placing a white plastic spoon into the dye bath. When you remove the spoon from the dye bath you can see the color change as it oxidizes. When this happens, your dye bath is ready.

7 Dampen the fabric and gently add it to the bath. Dye it for 2 to 30 minutes, depending on the color and desired depth of shade. Squeeze out any excess dye beneath the surface of the dye bath and then pull the fabric out. Don't let any dye drip back into the bath.

8 Rinse the fabric in room-temperature water and hang the fabric to oxidize for a minimum of 10 minutes.

9 Do a final wash to remove any of the vat dye that still rests on the fabric's surface. To do so, measure 1 capful of detergent into 2½ gallons (9.5 l) of boiling water. Submerge the fabric and allow it to simmer for about 10 minutes. Let the water cool, rinse, and hang to dry.

Discharging (Undyeing) Fabric

Taking the color out of fabric can be just as interesting as putting color in. Discharge dyeing is particularly attractive for those who don't need to know exactly what their results will be. Most colors will not discharge 100 percent, and often the colors don't even discharge in the same color family. You can always do test samples, but I have to admit, I like to wrap my cloth and throw it into a discharge bath just to see what comes out. My particular preference when discharging fabric is sueded rayon—I've never been disappointed in the rich results.

There are two basic recipes for discharging fabric. One uses bleach and the other uses Thiox. I prefer using Thiox for a couple of reasons. One is that I cannot stand the smell of bleach! Although Thiox does have a strong odor, it's not as strong as bleach and the smell doesn't linger. Also, I find that I do have a little more control when using Thiox. It works fairly quickly, but there is time to remove the fabric and stop the process. This isn't always the case with bleach. If bleach is left in the fiber, the chlorine seriously weakens it. It may also be difficult to obtain a given shade when over-dyeing. Both processes require the strict use of safety goggles, gloves, and a well-ventilated space. You may also want to use a cartridge respirator.

Discharging on Cellulose Fibers Using Thiox

What You Need

1 pound (.5 kg) of fabric

Burner

Several gallons (liters) water

1 large stainless steel pot

Plastic spoon

Thermometer

2½ teaspoons (12.5 ml) Thiox (thiourea dioxide)

2 tablespoons (30 ml) dye activator or soda ash

What You Do

1 Dampen the fabric and set aside.

2 On the burner, heat 2½ gallons (9.5 l) of water from 175° to 180°F (78° to 81°C) in the pot.

3 Add the Thiox and dye activator or soda ash.

4 Add the damp fabric and stir. The more you stir the bath, the more even your discharge results will be. Remove the fabric when you've reached the color you want.

5 Rinse the fabric well. It is ready to be re-dyed as desired.

Discharging Wool or Silk Using Thiox

What You Need

1 pound (.45 kg) of fabric

Burner

Several gallons (liters) water

2 large stainless steel pots

Plastic spoon

Thermometer

2½ teaspoons (12.5 ml) Thiox (thiourea dioxide)

1 tablespoon (15 ml) dye activator or soda ash

11 tablespoons (165 ml) white distilled vinegar or 1 tablespoon (15 ml) acetic acid

What You Do

1 Dampen the fabric and set aside.

2 Using the burner, heat 2½ gallons (9.5 l) of water from 175° to 180°F (78° to 81°C) in one of the pots.

3 Add the Thiox and dye activator or soda ash.

4 Immediately after making the bath, add the fabric. The more you stir the bath with the spoon, the more even your discharge results will be. Remove the fabric when you've reached the color you want.

5 To neutralize the reaction on wool or silk, combine 1 gallon (3.8 l) of warm water and the vinegar or acetic acid in another stainless steel pot. Soak the fabric for 10 to 15 minutes.

6 Rinse the fabric well. It is ready to be over-dyed as desired.

Discharging Cotton or Other Cellulose Fibers Using Bleach

What You Need

1 pound (.45 kg) of fabric

2 large, clean plastic buckets

Several gallons (liters) of water

1 teaspoon (5 ml) Anti-Chlor Concentrate

1 gallon (3.8 l) chlorine bleach, plus more if needed

Plastic spoon

What You Do

1 Dampen the fabric and set aside.

2 Make an Anti-Chlor bath by filling one of the buckets with 2½ gallons (9.5 l) of warm water. Thoroughly dissolve the Anti-Chlor in the water.

3 Pour 1 gallon (3.8 l) of bleach and 1 gallon (3.8 l) of water into the second bucket.

4 Add the fabric to the bleach bath. Remove it when you've reached the color you want. If you are unable to discharge the fabric to the appropriate degree, remove the fabric, add more bleach, and continue stirring. Never heat the bleach!

5 Soak the discharged fabric in the Anti-Chlor mixture for 5 minutes, stirring occasionally.

6 Rinse the fabric well in room-temperature water. It is ready to be over-dyed as desired.

Folding and Clamping

Preparing fabric by folding and clamping it may be the least mysterious and most immediate shibori process. It's easy, but can yield terrific results. The traditional Japanese folding-and-clamping method requires two boards to hold the folded fabric in place. The final design is created by the way the fabric extends beyond the boards, as well as by how much fabric is exposed.

Washers, bobbins, paper clips—even children's toys—can be used as resists in the folding and clamping process.

Use common items found at any hardware store for folding and clamping.

Tools & Supplies

Iron (optional)

Scoured fabric

Various types and sizes of clamps (C-clamps, spring clamps, binder clips, etc.)

Wood, plastic, or stainless steel objects in various shapes (2 of each)

The traditional method creates positive and negative patterns, yet it's difficult to discern which pattern is which. In the contemporary applications of folding and clamping, it can be quite easy to identify the positive and negative space.

Any fabric may be used for folding and clamping techniques. I prefer to use cotton, linen, or rayon and fiber-reactive dyes. This method creates incredibly tight barriers that won't allow fiber-reactive dyes to seep through easily. Because the clamps create these tight barriers, this technique produces very distinct patterns.

Folding

This process involves folding the fabric before it's clamped and dyed. Although ironing after folding really isn't necessary, I recommend it so your shibori lines are tight and even. If you're going for a less ordered look, then you can just smooth the fabric with your hands as you fold it.

To begin, make the folds in the cloth. The possibilities for this are endless. You'll see some common folds in this chapter, including accordion folds, which produce repetitive designs along the length of the fabric, and square folds that lend themselves to symmetrical designs. Triangle folds can produce the hexagonal design often seen in traditional shibori. (In traditional shibori, a fold that leaves triangle-shaped areas exposed to the dye may also be identified as a "triangle." You'll see both of these triangle techniques on pages 40 and 41.) Fabric folded into a cone can create a circular design. All of these folding techniques are illustrated, beginning on page 38.

Clamping

After folding and ironing, clamp the cloth in place. You have just as many options for clamping as you do for folding. You can clamp the fabric only once in the middle or numerous times-it just depends on how tight you want your final design to look.

You also have the option to experiment with different types of clamps. To create the shibori in this book, I primarily used spring clamps and C-clamps, both of which are readily available in the tools section of your hardware store. Each type of clamp leaves a different marking on the fabric, some with square edges and others with rounded borders, so you can use that to your design advantage. I like to use the same clamp on both sides of the fabric for uniformity.

After folding and clamping, dye the fabric as desired. I usually find that the most interesting pieces have been dyed more than once, building the color field with each dye bath.

Fold the cloth and press before you clamp.

Adding designs

In addition to creating patterns by folding, you can also make specific designs on the fabric by clamping different objects to it. The clamp tightens the object(s) against the fabric, creating a strong resist.

For this technique, you can use a wide variety of objects, including bobbins, washers, and blocks. I began my search for objects by digging through the kitchen junk drawer, moved on to a hardware store, and then to an office supply store. At the suggestion of a friend, I ended up raiding my son's block collection while he was out playing at a friend's house.

For example, hollow circles are created by items such as bobbins and washers, while solid circles are created by round blocks. I also stumbled onto some interesting items while wandering around in the hardware store, things like round plastic pieces from a closet organization system. And square blocks make solid squares, as you might imagine.

See examples of folding and clamping techniques on the pages that follow. You can incorporate these folds into your exploration of other forms of shibori, too.

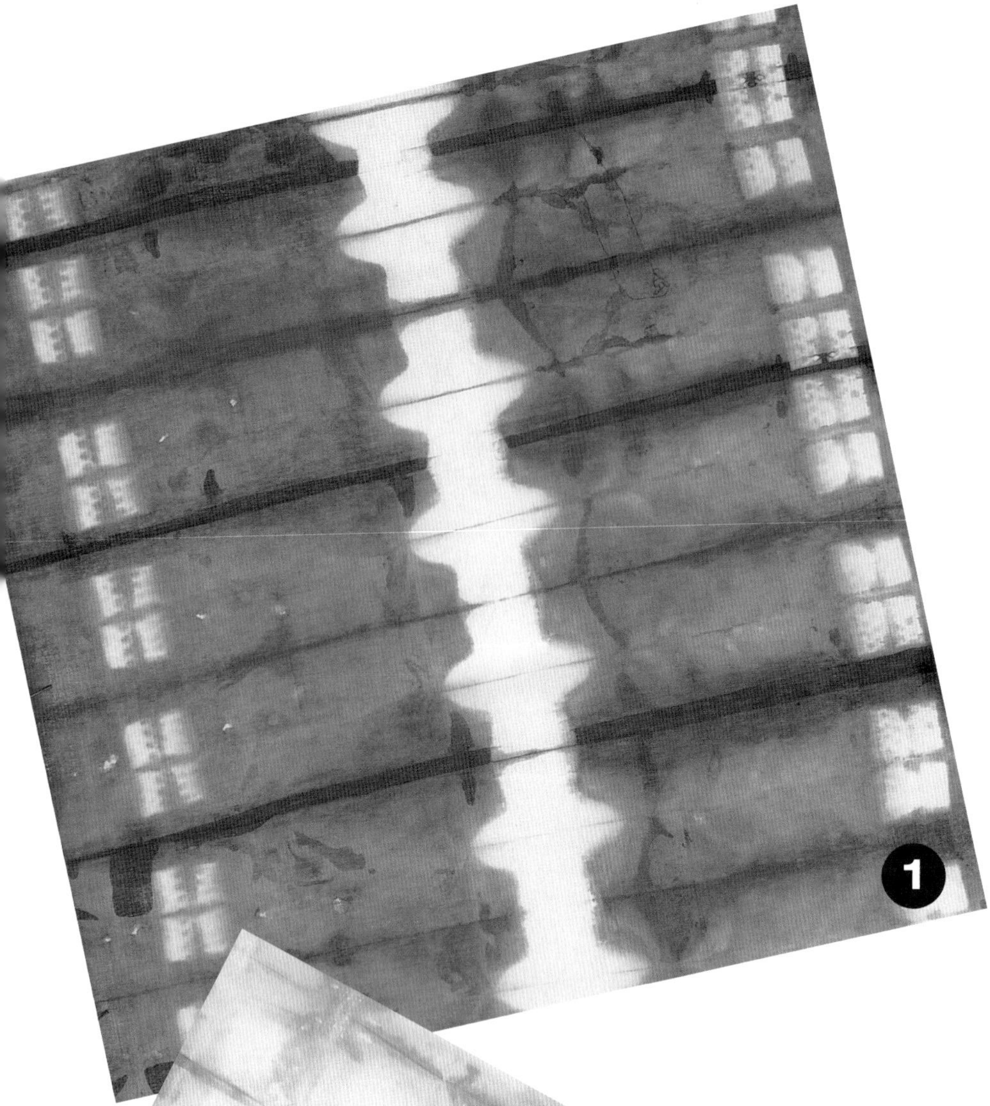

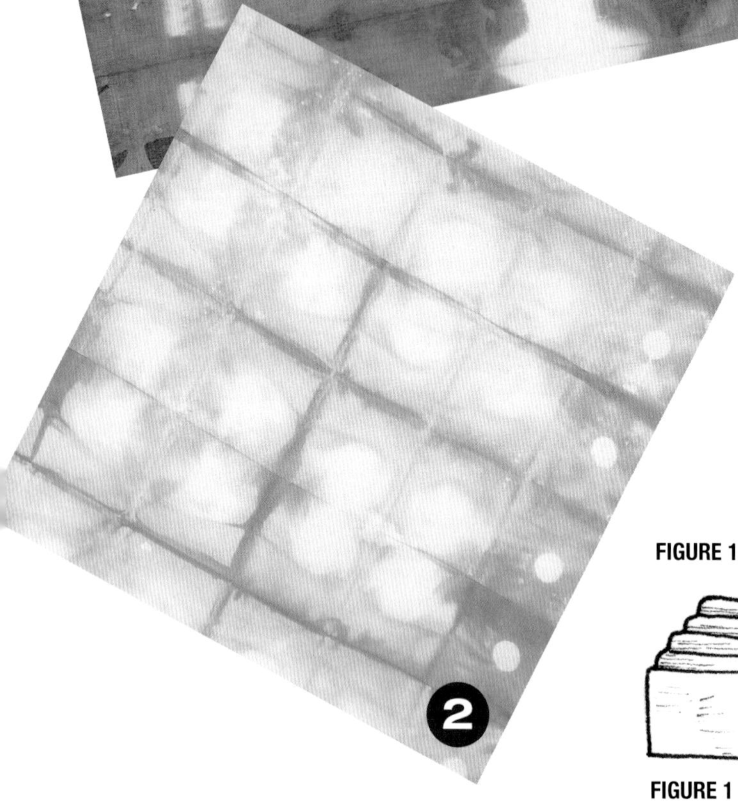

Accordion

Sample 1

I used an accordion fold on the swatch of white cotton organza you see in photo 1. The middle section was clamped between two shaped blocks, with a C-clamp. I put binder clips directly on the fabric before submerging it in an indigo dye bath. There's no need to treat these clamped pieces carefully when you're putting them in the dye bath—just dunk and go.

Sample 2

The swatch in photo 2 was also made with cotton organza. I used a series of blocks and C-clamps to keep the accordion folds in place and dyed it with vat dye. This produced a very different effect than seen in photo 1.

As you can see, the accordion fold is very useful for repetition of your design. Also, there is no deep interior when the cloth is folded this way, so that the dye tends to reach all areas of the cloth evenly.

FIGURE 1. *An accordion fold*

FIGURE 1

DYER'S NOTES
Squares

Sample 3

This piece of silk brocade was found in the wedding section of an elegant fabric store. I purchased ¼ yard (22.9 cm)—all I could afford—and took it straight to the studio. I folded this piece into a square, using three folds and alternating the directions. Then, I clamped one block on each side of the fabric with the C-clamp. It was then dyed in an acid dye bath.

It's easy to see that folding fabric into a square before dyeing it creates a symmetrical pattern. Sometimes, the lines become less sharp if a large piece of cloth is folded too many times. Generally, the fewer times a cloth is folded into squares, the stronger the images are.

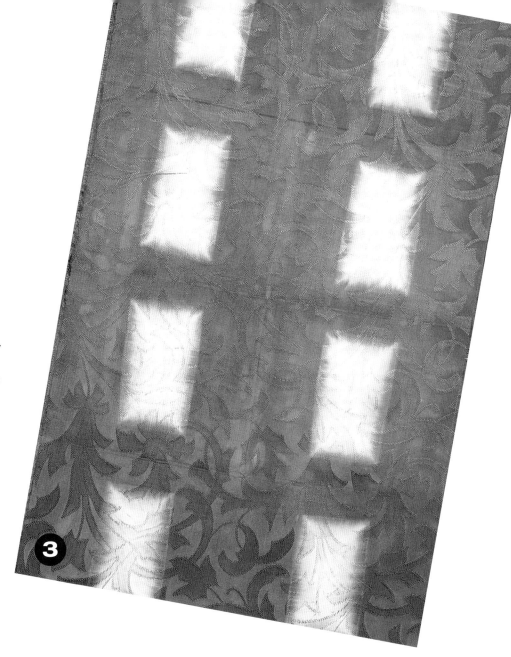

FIGURES 2 AND 3. *A square fold*

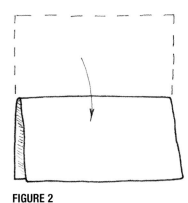

FIGURE 2

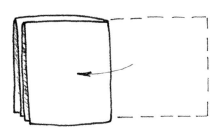

FIGURE 3

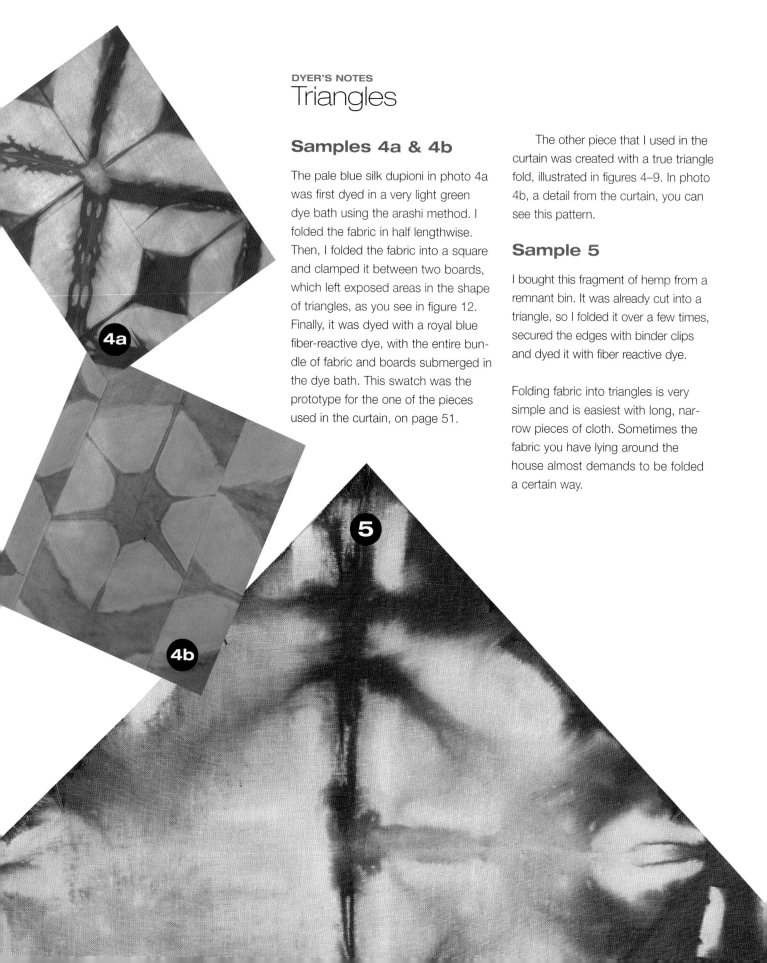

Triangles

Samples 4a & 4b

The pale blue silk dupioni in photo 4a was first dyed in a very light green dye bath using the arashi method. I folded the fabric in half lengthwise. Then, I folded the fabric into a square and clamped it between two boards, which left exposed areas in the shape of triangles, as you see in figure 12. Finally, it was dyed with a royal blue fiber-reactive dye, with the entire bundle of fabric and boards submerged in the dye bath. This swatch was the prototype for the one of the pieces used in the curtain, on page 51.

The other piece that I used in the curtain was created with a true triangle fold, illustrated in figures 4–9. In photo 4b, a detail from the curtain, you can see this pattern.

Sample 5

I bought this fragment of hemp from a remnant bin. It was already cut into a triangle, so I folded it over a few times, secured the edges with binder clips and dyed it with fiber reactive dye.

Folding fabric into triangles is very simple and is easiest with long, narrow pieces of cloth. Sometimes the fabric you have lying around the house almost demands to be folded a certain way.

FIGURES 4, 5, 6, 7, 8, AND 9. *Here are the steps to make a triangle fold; it produces the hexagonal design often seen in traditional shibori, called tortoiseshell. After the first fold, turn the fabric upside down and continue folding the triangle.*

FIGURES 10, 11, AND 12. *This series of folds leaves a triangle-shaped area of fabric outside the resist (the boards). Fold the fabric into a nice square by draping the fabric back and forth, as in figure 10, before clamping it in place. The resulting fabric actually has a circular quality. In traditional shibori, this is also referred to as triangles, even though the fold is square.*

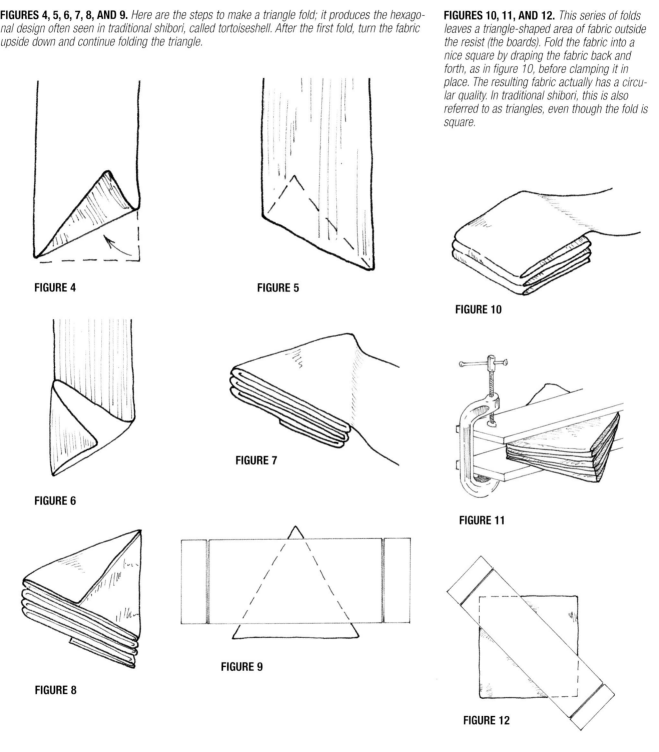

FIGURE 4

FIGURE 5

FIGURE 10

FIGURE 6

FIGURE 7

FIGURE 11

FIGURE 8

FIGURE 9

FIGURE 12

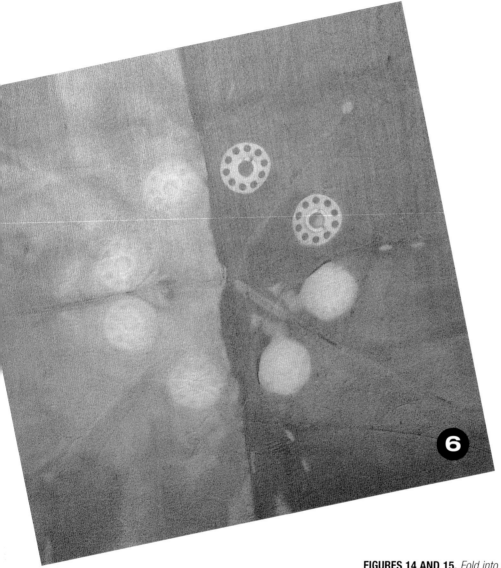

Cones

Sample 6

This silk charmeuse swatch was folded into a cone shape and then clamped, with a sewing machine bobbin between the fabric and the clamp on each side. It was then dyed in fiber-reactive dye. You can see how the interior sections of the cone are less clear than the areas that were directly in contact with the bobbins.

Unlike other forms of folding fabric, the cone shape will create a circular pattern on the cloth. The cone shape is useful in other shibori techniques, too, such as stitching and gathering and bound resists, but it's used less often in folding and clamping.

FIGURES 14 AND 15. *Fold into a cone as shown; this fold can be either clamped or stitched in place.*

FIGURE 14

FIGURE 15

Hollow Circles

Sample 7

This piece of gold silk dupioni had red embroidered circles on it when I bought it. I thought it would be fun to mimic the embroidered circles with a dyed pattern, so I first folded the fabric in half widthwise, and then widthwise once again. Then I folded it lengthwise, to make a tidy square, and used giant washers and C-clamps to clamp the fabric. I finished it off in a fiber-reactive dye bath. You can easily see which squares were on the outside and thus exposed to the dye—it's the second group of circles below the top.

Sample 8

The piece of silk in photo 8 was cross-dyed, with two colors visible from the warp and weft yarns that were different shades. This iridescent sheen is now only visible in the undyed areas, because once dyed the warp and weft are the same color, of course. This fabric was folded into a square several times, and then I applied bobbins and C-clamps before putting it in an acid dye.

Sample 9

A completely different effect is shown in photo 9. This cotton organza swatch was red when I purchased it. I folded it lengthwise, and then across several times, before placing two small washers near a corner of the fold. I clamped them in place, and then discharged the fabric with Thiox. The resulting arrangement of shapes results from the placement of the washers. If they had been centered on the cloth, there would have been an all-over pattern.

Hollow circles are great fun to work with because you get two sets of circles, one interior and one exterior (or one positive and one negative, if you will). Objects that will form these circles are easy to find; any washer will do.

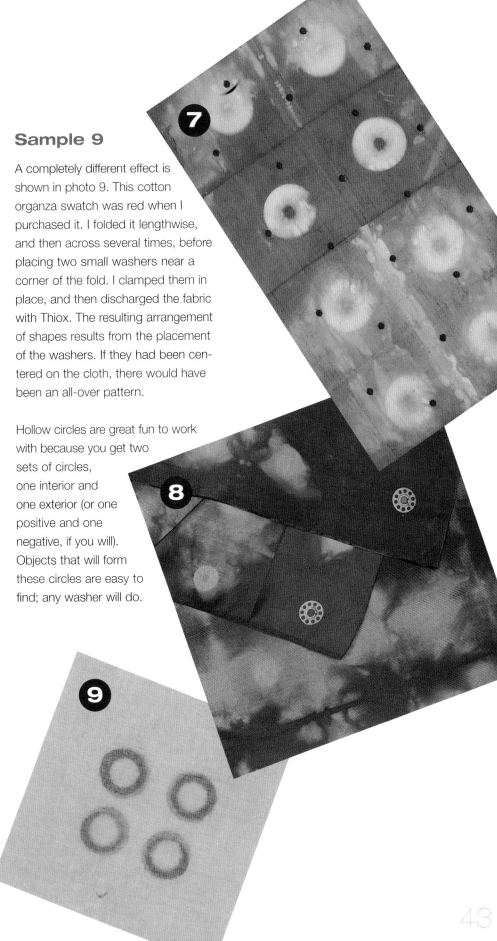

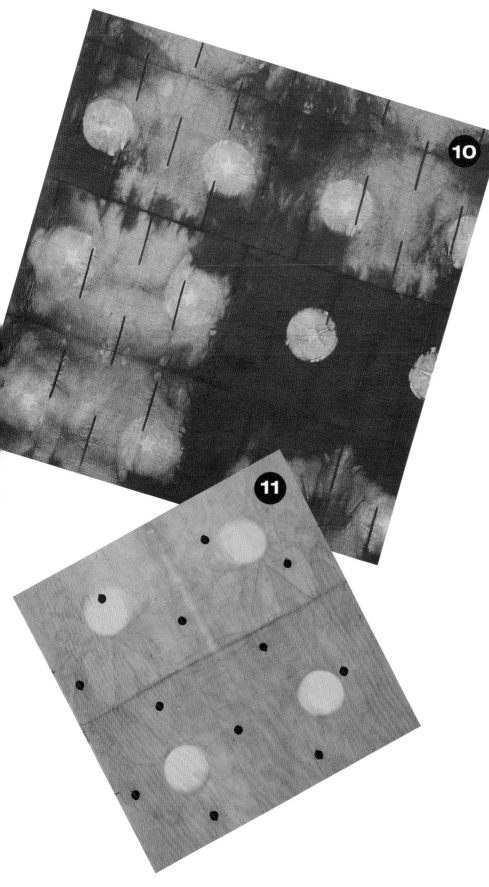

Solid Circles

Sample 10

The basis for the swatch in photo 10 was a gold silk dupioni, embroidered with red stripes. While scavenging for resists before dyeing, I found a package of plastic gizmos in a kitchen drawer. (They were supposed to be used to add another pole in a closet, but I sent them straight to the studio.) There's a slight star-shaped pattern on the plastic pieces that was a surprising addition to the finished product. I applied them with C-clamps, but I had no idea that they were clamped tightly enough to retain that design. Keep your eyes open for intriguing objects that can be used as resists. I used acid dye for this sample.

Sample 11

Here's another piece of gold silk dupioni, but this one had embroidered red dots and seemed perfect for round resists. I folded the fabric twice, placed two round blocks in the center of the folds, and secured them in place with C-clamps. This swatch was dyed with fiber-reactive dye.

As you can probably tell, using solid circles as your resist creates a bolder look for your completed project. The positive and negative spaces are more easily determined, and the fabric tends to have a real foreground and background.

Solid Squares

Sample 12

I folded this square silk scarf into a tri-angle and repeated the triangle fold several more times. I clamped blocks in place with a C-clamp and then dyed the scarf with acid dye. I chose this bright yellow dye color even though it's not in my "auto palette." Try colors you don't expect to like every now and then—you may be surprised, as I was.

Sample 13

The square blocks used in photo 13 created a completely different swatch. This white piece of cotton velveteen was folded in half, and then folded in half again. Two square blocks were placed off-center (closer to one edge than another) and secured with a C-clamp. I used fiber-reactive dye.

Like solid circles, objects that leave solid square patterns are usually easy to find around the house. Sometimes you don't even need an object—some spring clamps have square tips and leave square marks with nothing between them and the fabric they clamp.

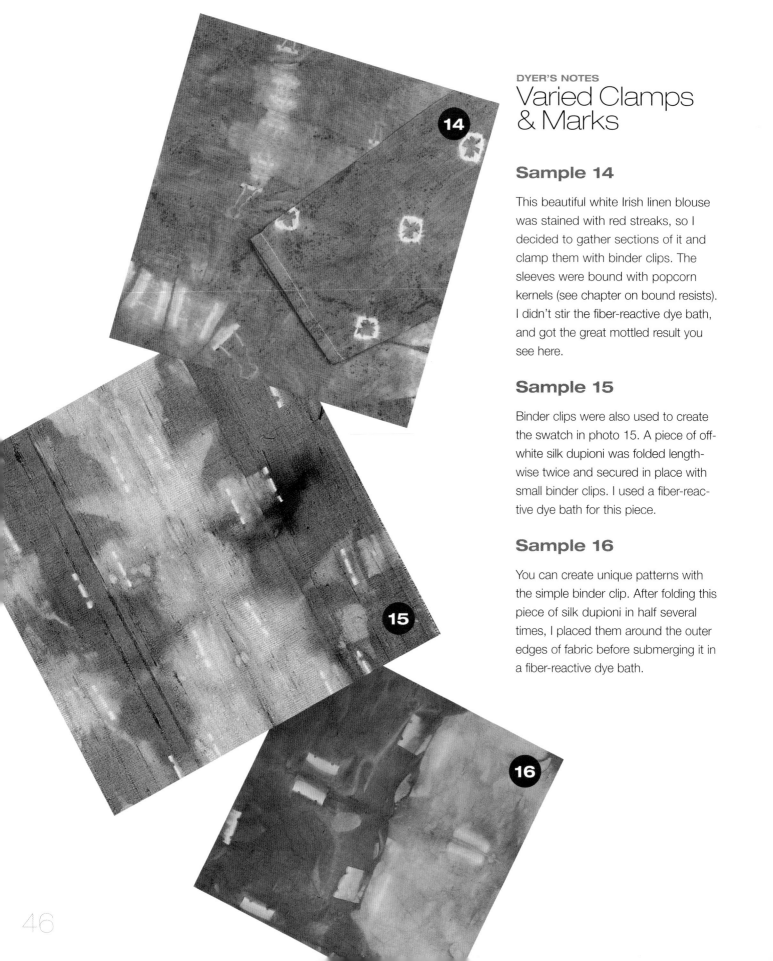

Varied Clamps & Marks

Sample 14

This beautiful white Irish linen blouse was stained with red streaks, so I decided to gather sections of it and clamp them with binder clips. The sleeves were bound with popcorn kernels (see chapter on bound resists). I didn't stir the fiber-reactive dye bath, and got the great mottled result you see here.

Sample 15

Binder clips were also used to create the swatch in photo 15. A piece of off-white silk dupioni was folded length-wise twice and secured in place with small binder clips. I used a fiber-reactive dye bath for this piece.

Sample 16

You can create unique patterns with the simple binder clip. After folding this piece of silk dupioni in half several times, I placed them around the outer edges of fabric before submerging it in a fiber-reactive dye bath.

Sample 17

In photo 17, you see how the objects you clamp onto the fabric affect the final outcome. This cotton velveteen was clamped between two very similar, but not identical, wooden blocks and secured with a C-clamp. It was finished with a fiber-reactive dye bath.

Sample 18

This swatch of purple sueded rayon was folded lengthwise, and then folded several times across. Two oddly shaped blocks were secured with C-clamps and dyed with vat dyes. Notice that the vat dyes replaced the purple with the red, the color of the dye. This was one of the first times I worked with vat dyes, and I loved the color discharge process.

Sample 19

You may want to visit a toy store to look for resists. In photo 19, I used blocks with human shapes and C-clamps to create this interesting swatch. It was dyed with fiber-reactive dye.

Sample 20

Lastly, I used two bridge-shaped blocks for the lovely swatch in photo 20. This cotton fabric was also secured with C-clamps and then dyed with fiber-reactive dyes.

A WORD OF CAUTION

Although I used blocks from my son's collection to create many pieces of shibori, he had outgrown them and I had no intention of returning them to his toy box. Please be aware that these objects *should not* be used as toys after they've gone through the dyeing process.

Revitalized Napkins

I bought these napkins and used them for several years. They were beginning to look a little dingy, so I gave them a shibori facelift.

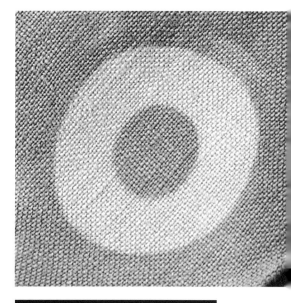

What You Do

1 Fold the napkin twice so the four corners come together.

2 Place two of the washers on the outsides of the napkin and one in the middle of the four layers.

3 Clamp the washers tightly with the C-clamps.

4 Dye the fabric in the dye bath, following the instructions on page 25 for dyeing with fiber-reactive dyes.

5 Rinse the napkins until the water runs clear. Release the clamps.

6 Block the napkins, returning them to their original size and shape, and iron to dry.

7 To complete the facelift, embellish with beads as desired.

What You Need

Linen napkins

3 large washers per napkin

Small C-clamps

Terra cotta fiber-reactive dye bath

Iron

Variety of beads

Beading thread and needle

Fold-and-Clamp Window Panel

This easy-to-sew window panel was designed to fold up to let in light. If you prefer not to use the panel as a window treatment, it can easily become a wall hanging.

What You Need

Scissors

2 pieces of light blue silk dupioni fabric, each 60 x 44 inches (152.4 x 111.8 cm)

4 C-clamps

8 wooden blocks, 2 x 10 x ¼ inches (5.1 x 25.4 x 0.6 cm) each

Blue fiber-reactive dye bath

Iron

Straight pins

Sewing machine

Sewing thread, blue

Sewing needle

24 inches (61 cm) of ¼-inch (0.6 cm) blue organza ribbon

3 light blue transparent 1-inch (2.5 cm) glass buttons

What You Do

Use a ½-inch (1.3 cm) seam allowance unless otherwise noted.

1 With scissors, cut one of the fabric pieces into four 11 x 60-inch (27.9 x 152.4 cm) strips.

2 Fold two of the pieces into traditional Japanese hexagonal pattern (figures 4–9 on page 41).

Secure the folds by clamping the wooden blocks to each side of the fabric.

Fold the remaining two pieces in half lengthwise and then in a series of accordion folds (figures 10–12 on page 41).

Secure the folds by clamping the wooden blocks on each side of the fabric.

3 Dye the fabric in the blue dye bath, following the instructions on page 25 for dyeing with fiber-reactive dyes. Rinse until the water runs clear and unclamp the cloth. Immediately rinse the cloth again to make sure that all excess dye is removed. Dry and iron the cloth.

4 Pin the strips of the dyed fabric together, right sides facing. Stitch one long edge of the strips together. Press the seam open. Repeat until all the dyed strips are sewn together.

5 Pin the dyed fabric to the un-dyed piece of silk, right sides together. Stitch along the sides and the bottom.

6 Turn the window panel right side out. Carefully fold the top over 1 inch (2.5 cm) and press the fold in place. Fold the top over again 3 inches (7.6 cm) and press it in place. Pin the fold and use a needle and thread to hemstitch the fabric in place, forming a casing.

7 Cut the organza ribbon into three equal pieces and fold one piece in half, aligning the ends. Sew the loose ends of it to the back of the panel, 1 inch (2.5 cm) in from the right-hand bottom corner. The result should be a 3-inch (7.6 cm) loop hanging from the bottom of the panel. Repeat for the left-hand bottom corner and for the middle of the bottom.

8 Use a needle and thread to sew the buttons to the top of the panel. They should sit 3 inches (7.6 cm) from the top on the front of the panel, and correspond to the ribbon loop placement.

9 To use the panel, place a curtain rod through the casing made in step 6. To let light in, loop the ribbons around the buttons.

Arashi

Scarf made of China silk and dyed with fabric paint

The term arashi is the Japanese word for "storm." It also describes the chaotic designs on a piece of shibori cloth, reminiscent of rain blown by the wind. Arashi shibori is created by wrapping: first wrapping the fabric around a pipe, then wrapping the fabric with ties that act as resists. Finally, the pipe is dipped into a dye bath (or the fabric can be painted with fabric paint or thickened dye). The process can be repeated over and over again so the fabric reflects many levels of color. I find arashi to be very gratifying because the outcome is immediate. Once the cloth has been dyed, you just unwrap the fabric and voilà! You're holding a gorgeous piece of cloth.

Tools & Supplies

Scoured fabric

PVC pipe

Masking tape

Various ties

Iron (optional)

Dye bath (or optional fabric paint)

One of the most beautiful qualities of arashi shibori cloth is its rhythm. Because you're making repetitive wraps with the ties, the end product has an elegant pattern. To fully capitalize on that effect, I like to work with silk because the flow of the fabric emphasizes the flowing arashi design.

Many materials, including rickrack and rubber bands, are suitable for tying or binding arashi fabric.

Attach the Fabric

Begin your arashi project by deciding how you will attach the fabric to the PVC pipe, as well as how you will wrap it on the pipe. Your decision will make a big difference in the outcome of the process. For example, if you choose to wrap the fabric around the pipe several times, the inner layer of cloth will absorb less dye than the outer layer will. And although arashi is, at its heart, a somewhat random process, you can plan the designs to a certain degree by pushing and wrapping the fabric at regular intervals.

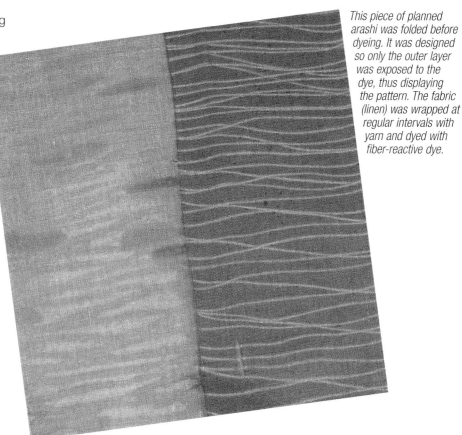

This piece of planned arashi was folded before dyeing. It was designed so only the outer layer was exposed to the dye, thus displaying the pattern. The fabric (linen) was wrapped at regular intervals with yarn and dyed with fiber-reactive dye.

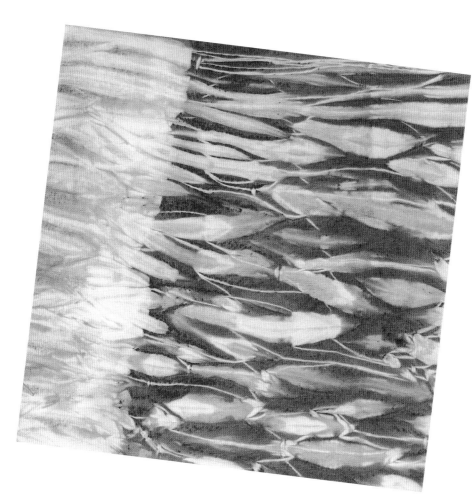

Swatch made from cotton, using fiber reactive dye; this arashi piece was randomly wrapped around a pole with a small diameter.

You can simply cover the pipe with the fabric, in which case you would secure it at the end of the pipe with a small piece of masking tape (figure 1). You can also attach it so it spirals down the pipe (figure 2), which creates diagonal designs. Regardless of where you attach the tape, remove it before you dye the fabric, or it will act as an additional resist.

To determine which kind of designs you like best, I suggest making sample cloths using two different sizes of PVC pipe. I find that it's easier to work with pipe with a diameter of about 1½ inches (3.8 cm) or more.

FIGURE 1

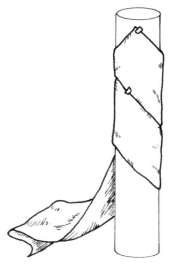

FIGURE 2

Random Wrapping

The second part of this process is wrapping the fabric with ties. You may want to revisit the information about ties on page 22, because the type of tie you choose will affect your design.

You can wrap the ties in a completely random fashion. After securing the cloth to the pipe with tape, slowly turn the pipe while wrapping a tie tightly around the fabric. Tie a square knot to hold it in place. Leave a 6-inch (15.2 cm) or so tail so you can tie the other end to it when you're finished wrapping. Your tie should be fairly long—5 feet (4.6 m) or so. I like to use yarn from a large cone and just cut it when I'm finished wrapping.

Continue to wrap the tie around the cloth from the same direction (photo 1), pushing as you go so that the entire piece of cloth is bunched to a finished length that will fit inside your dye container, about 6 to 8 inches (15.2 to 20.3 cm). It's easiest to finish off by tying one end of the tie to the other with a square knot (photo 2). After the last turn of the pipe, be sure to push the cloth so your final wrap will also be submerged when you lower the pipe into the dye bath.

For your first random project, make sure that each time you turn the pipe you wrap the ties in different ways (at an angle, overlapping each other, etc.). Consider letting some of the cloth poke through at different intervals throughout the wrapping. When you've finished wrapping, you can also pull small sections of cloth free from the ties to add to the random effect (photo 3). If you want, you could also wrap the entire pipe again with more ties.

Lastly, for a truly random effect, bunch the fabric together so it wrinkles before you wrap it with ties.

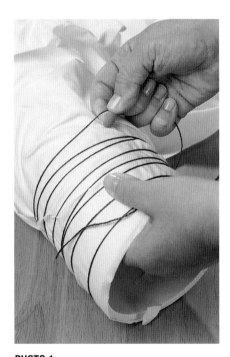

PHOTO 1

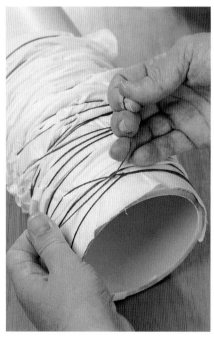

PHOTO 2

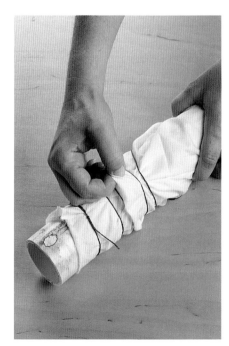

PHOTO 3

Planned Wrapping

Although it can be very difficult to plan an arashi piece of cloth, it's not impossible. To do so, wrap ties around the cloth so they're spaced consistently, and at the same time, push the cloth up the pipe at regular intervals. The combination creates an even pattern. Folding is also a type of planning: to get a very orderly look, iron the fabric into accordion pleats before attaching it to the pipe.

Over-Dyeing

If you wish, you may over-dye (page 24) your cloth. Because it's a relatively easy technique, arashi lends itself well to this dyeing method. To do it, rinse your cloth thoroughly after the first dye bath and hang to dry. Start the entire process again using the same cloth.

There are many directions you can go in when over-dyeing arashi shibori cloth. You can use the same color over and over to create several depths of the same shade, or layer colors as you like. And, of course, you can always discharge the cloth.

These shibori techniques are illustrated in the pages that follow. Some of them use folding techniques from the Folding and Clamping chapter (page 35).

Tip

One of my favorite tricks in creating ties for arashi shibori is to dye yarn without rinsing it clear. Then I let the yarn dry completely. I use the yarn to secure the cloth to the pipe, and the dye from the yarn transfers to the fabric, leaving interesting marks, as you see above.

1

2

Random Wrapping

Sample 1

I really loved the way this silk velvet swatch retained the lines from the cotton yarn that was used as the resist. The texture formed from the pile of the velvet was a terrific surprise, and I'll never iron it out. This piece was dyed in an acid dye bath.

Sample 2

Another dramatic example of simple arashi is seen in photo 2. This bright yellow swatch of silk charmeuse was randomly wrapped with yarn and dyed in a red acid dye bath. It's reminiscent of an electrical storm, so it seems to reflect arashi's origins.

FIGURES 1 AND 2. *You can simply bunch up the fabric and bind it to the pole in a random fashion.*

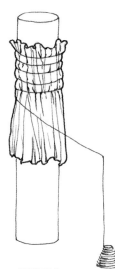

FIGURE 1   **FIGURE 2**

Sample 3

The effect seen here is a bit more subtle than swatch 2, but it is also made from silk charmeuse and acid dye.

Sample 4

Speaking of subtle, my first attempt with the swatch in photo 4 was so faint that I repeated the dye process. This silk charmeuse sample was randomly wrapped around the pole, and then randomly wrapped with yarn. It was bunched in some places—yet left untouched in others—and then dyed with acid dye.

FIGURES 3 AND 4. *You can dye more than one piece of fabric at a time and tape them together. After you've wrapped the cloth with ties, remember to remove the tape so it doesn't act as a resist.*

Sample 5

Finally, you can also employ the arashi technique without using dye. The China silk blank scarf in photo 5 was wrapped randomly on the pole, and the yarn wrapped around it in a similar fashion. To further enhance the random quality of the piece, I painted fabric dye on the tied piece and let it dry on the pole.

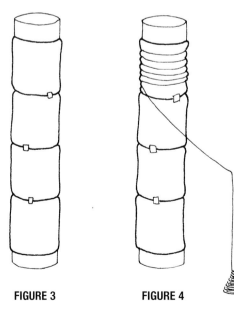

FIGURE 3   **FIGURE 4**

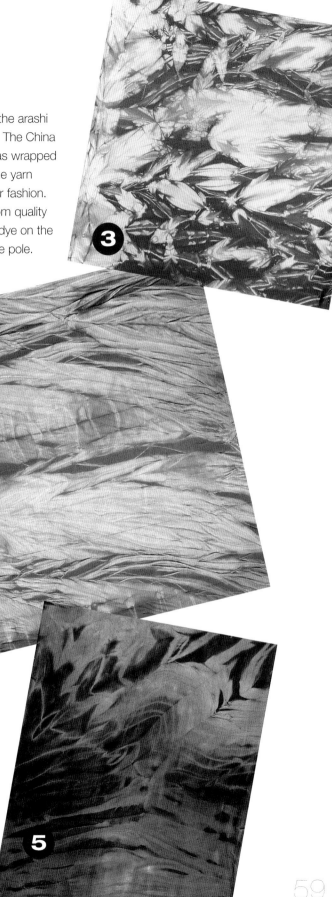

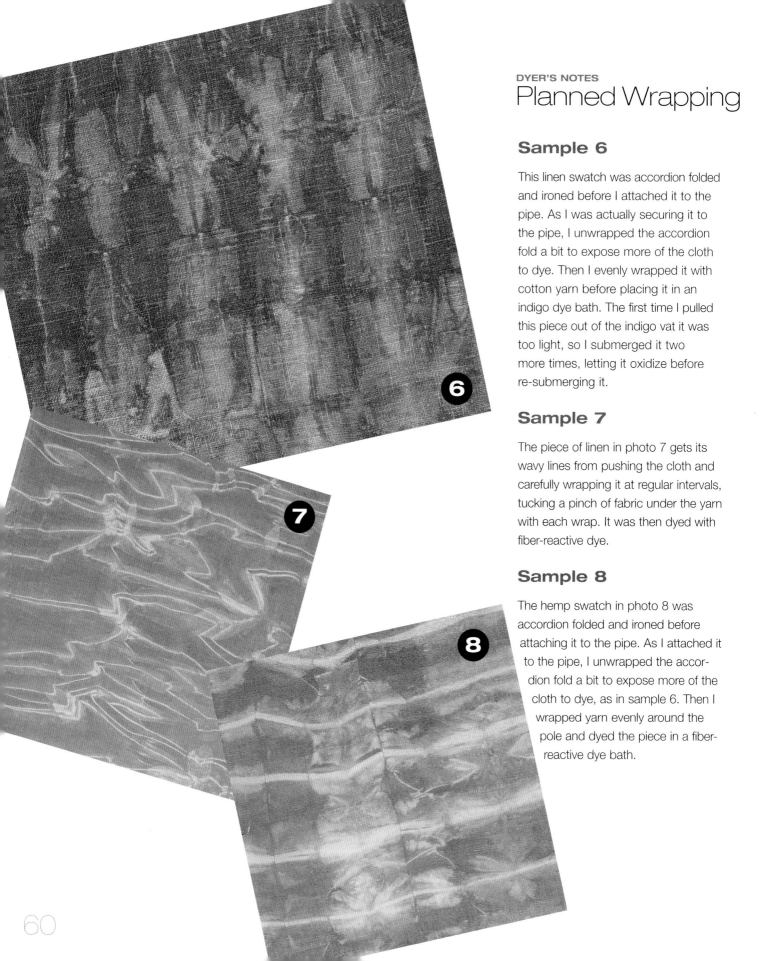

Planned Wrapping

Sample 6

This linen swatch was accordion folded and ironed before I attached it to the pipe. As I was actually securing it to the pipe, I unwrapped the accordion fold a bit to expose more of the cloth to dye. Then I evenly wrapped it with cotton yarn before placing it in an indigo dye bath. The first time I pulled this piece out of the indigo vat it was too light, so I submerged it two more times, letting it oxidize before re-submerging it.

Sample 7

The piece of linen in photo 7 gets its wavy lines from pushing the cloth and carefully wrapping it at regular intervals, tucking a pinch of fabric under the yarn with each wrap. It was then dyed with fiber-reactive dye.

Sample 8

The hemp swatch in photo 8 was accordion folded and ironed before attaching it to the pipe. As I attached it to the pipe, I unwrapped the accordion fold a bit to expose more of the cloth to dye, as in sample 6. Then I wrapped yarn evenly around the pole and dyed the piece in a fiber-reactive dye bath.

Samples 9a & 9b

The last two examples demonstrate how different fabrics react to the same dye. In photo 9a, a piece of cotton was folded in half, and then in an accordion fold, before it was ironed and wrapped with yarn. The swatch in photo 9b, silk georgette, was placed in same dye bath as sample 9a; it was folded in half before being attached to the pipe and wrapped at regular intervals. Both swatches were dyed in vat dye.

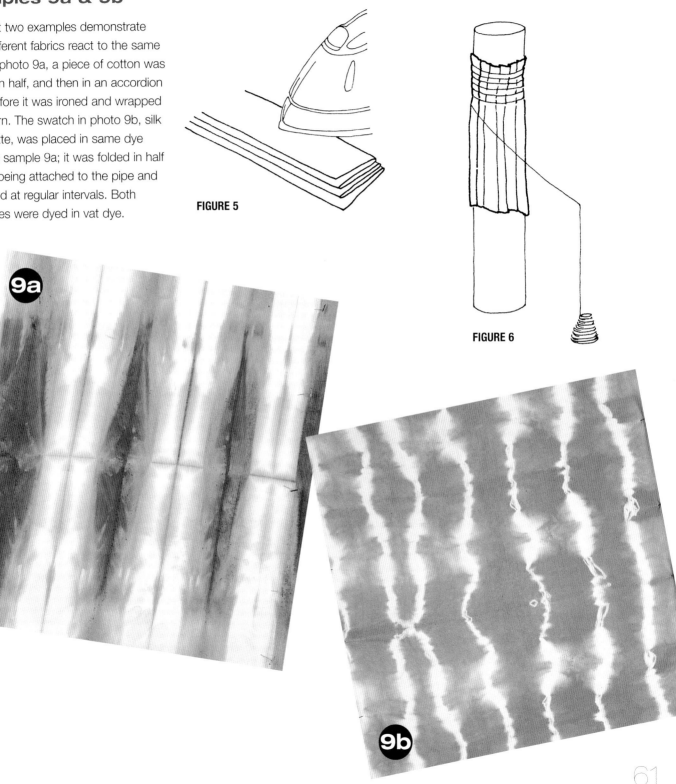

FIGURE 5

FIGURE 6

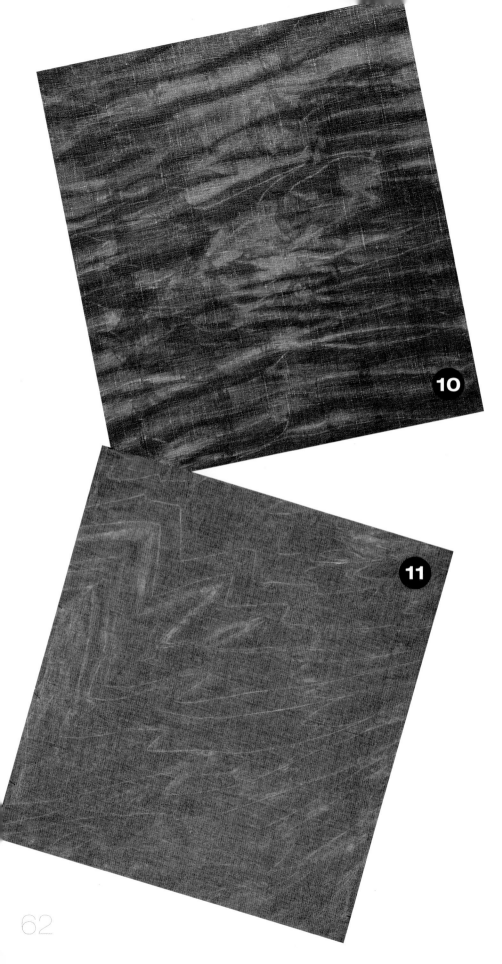

Over-Dyeing

Sample 10

This piece in photo 10 was planned and over-dyed. The swatch was made from light blue linen that was dyed with dark blue fiber-reactive dye, and then over-dyed in forest green fiber-reactive dye. This was designed by carefully pushing the fabric along the pipe about 1 inch (2.5 cm) between each wrap of the cotton yarn.

Sample 11

I used wispy cotton organza for this swatch. It was randomly wrapped on the pipe with yarn and dyed with raspberry fiber-reactive dye. Then, it was randomly wrapped and over-dyed in violet fiber-reactive dye.

Arashi Handbags

Rebecca Manske used some of my fabrics to design and sew these striking handbags. She used several fabrics that had each been dyed a little differently.

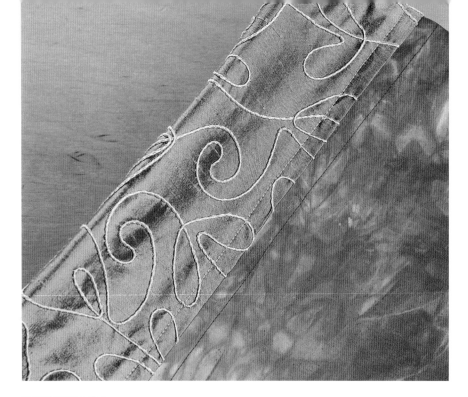

HANDBAG Nº 1

Pink Arashi Bag

What You Do

Use a ¹⁄₂-inch (1.3 cm) seam allowance unless otherwise noted.

1 Cut two pieces of the handle fabric and two pieces of the interfacing, each 4 x 20 inches (10.2 x 50.8 cm). Following the manufacturer's directions, fuse the interfacing to each of the handle fabric pieces. Fold each handle (interfacing sides together) in half lengthwise and press; then fold the raw edges in to the center fold and press again. Topstitch along the edges.

2 Cut two pieces of the shibori fabric, each 8 x 13 inches (20.3 x 33 cm), per template A.

3 Cut two pieces of the contrasting fabric, each 5¼ x 13 inches (13.3 x 33 cm), with 1¾-inch (4.4 cm) corners cut out of the bottom, per template B.

4 Cut two pieces of fusible fleece, each 12¼ x 13 inches (31.1 x 33 cm), with 1¾-inch (4.4 cm) corners cut out of bottom, per template C.

5 With right sides facing, pin and sew the lower edge of the shibori pieces to the upper edge of the contrasting fabric pieces. Press the seam. Fuse one piece of the fleece to the wrong side of these pieces. Topstitch approximately ⅜ inch (1 cm) above and below the seam, as shown above.

6 With the right sides facing, stitch the front and back of the bag together at the side and bottom seams, leaving the corners open (figure 1). Fold to align the side and bottom seams and stitch the corners together (figure 2).

7 Place the needlepoint canvas in the bottom of the bag and hand stitch the canvas to both ends.

8 Turn the bag right side out. Pin the handles to the outside of the bag, raw edges together, and stitch.

Scissors

⅝ yard (0.6 m) of contrasting fabric for the handle and the bottom of the bag

¼ yard (0.2 m) of firm fusible backing/interfacing for the handle

Iron

Sewing machine

Thread to match the fabrics

⅜ yard (0.3 m) of shibori fabric

⅜ yard (0.3 m) of fusible fleece

Straight pins

1 piece of plastic needlepoint canvas, 3¼ x 8½ inches (8.3 x 21.6 cm)

Sewing needle

⅜ yard (0.3 m) of coordinating fabric for the lining and interior pocket

1 no-sew ⅝-inch (1.6 cm) magnetic snap

Templates on page 125

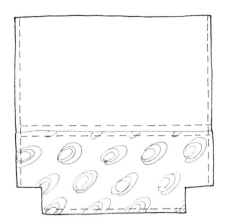

FIGURE 1

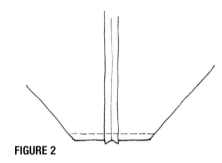

FIGURE 2

9 To make the pocket for the lining, cut one piece of lining fabric 11 x 6 inches (27.9 x 15.2 cm). Fold it in half horizontally with the right sides together and press. Stitch around the three sides of the pocket, leaving a 3-inch (7.6 cm) gap in the bottom. Clip the corners and turn the pocket right side out through the gap. Press. Topstitch along the top of the pocket below the fold.

10 Cut two pieces of lining fabric, each 12¼ x 13 inches (31.1 x 33 cm), with 1¾-inch (4.4 cm) corners cut from bottom, per template C. Center and pin the pocket to one of the pieces of lining fabric (it should sit about 3 inches [7.6 cm] in from the top). Stitch it in place. With the right sides together, stitch the two pieces of lining fabric

together, first down the sides and then across the bottom, leaving a 6-inch (15.2 cm) gap in the middle. Leave the corners open as in step 6, then fold and stitch the corners after you've sewn the sides and bottom, also as in step 6.

11 To reinforce the snap, cut two pieces of interfacing each 2 x 3 inches (5.1 x 7.6 cm). Fuse each piece to the wrong sides of the lining approximately ¾ inch (1.9 cm) from the top, centering each between the side seams.

12 Following the manufacturer's directions, position and insert the snap 2 inches (5.1 cm) in from the top of the lining, centered between the side seams.

13 Slip the bag into the lining so the right sides are together and the handles are tucked between the lining and the bag. Align the top edges and stitch, using a ⅝-inch (1.5 cm) seam allowance.

14 Turn the bag right side out through the opening in the lining. Stitch the lining closed and tuck it inside the bag.

15 Pin the bag and lining together and topstitch, making one line of topstitching ⅜ inch (1 cm) from the top of the bag, and a second line ⅜ inch (1 cm) away from the first, as shown above.

Patchwork Bag

What You Do

Use a ½-inch (1.3 cm) seam allowance unless otherwise noted.

1 For the handles, cut two strips from the shibori scraps and two pieces of the interfacing, each 2 x 13 inches (5.1 x 33 cm). Following the manufacturer's directions, fuse the interfacing to the wrong side of each of the handle pieces. Fold each handle (interfacing sides together) in half lengthwise and press; then fold the raw edges in to the center fold and press again. Topstitch along the edges.

2 Stitch the remaining shibori scraps together to form a fabric collage. Cut two panels out of the collage, each 10 x 9¼ inches (25.4 x 23.5 cm). These will be the front and the back of the bag.

3 Cut two pieces of fusible fleece, each 10 x 9¼ inches (25.4 x 23.5 cm), per template D. Fuse each piece to the wrong side of the fabric panels.

4 With right sides facing, stitch together the sides and bottom of the two panels.

5 Turn the bag right side out. Pin the handles to the outside of the bag, raw edges together. Stitch, using a ⅝-inch (1.5 cm) seam allowance.

6 Cut two pieces of lining fabric, each 10 x 9¼ inches (25.4 x 23.5 cm). With the right sides together, stitch the two pieces of lining fabric together, first down the sides and then across the bottom, leaving a 4-inch (10 cm) gap in the middle.

7 Slip the bag into the lining so the right sides are together and the handles are between the lining and the bag. Align the top edges and stitch.

8 Turn the bag right side out through the opening in the lining. Stitch the lining closed. Tuck the lining inside the bag.

9 Pin the bag and lining together and topstitch, making one line of topstitching ⅜ inch (1 cm) from the top of the bag, and a second line ⅜ inch (1 cm) away from the first, as shown in step 15 of the Pink Arashi Bag.

NOTE

It's important to do an ironing test run on small swatches of the fabrics you'll use for your bag because you'll be fusing them. If you're using silk, as in these projects, you may need to keep your iron temperature fairly low. But you really need only a light bond between your interfacing/fusible fleece and the fabric— the remaining stitching will hold it in place. That said, some fabrics might not be compatible with fusibles, so you'll want to choose a sew-in equivalent.

What You Need

Scissors

Shibori cloth scraps, enough to make two 2 x 13 inch (5.1 x 33 cm) handles and two 10 x 9¼-inch (25.4 x 23.5 cm) pieced panels

⅛ yard (0.1 m) of firm iron-on backing/interfacing for the handle, 44 inches (111.8 cm) wide

Iron

Sewing machine

Sewing thread to match the fabric

⅜ yard (0.3 m) of fusible fleece

Straight pins

⅜ yard (0.3 m) of coordinating fabric for the lining

Template on page 125

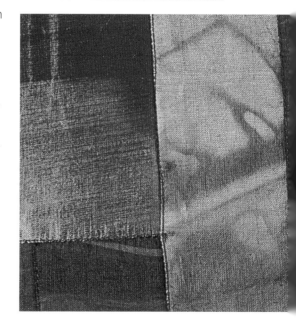

Bound Resists

The bound-resist technique is probably the most commonly recognized shibori method, as most tie-dyed T-shirts are created this way. As the name suggests, bound-resist shibori involves gathering part of the fabric and binding it with something that serves as the resist.

Creating bound resists is one of my favorite things to do. It's an easy technique—you can even do it while hanging out with your friends and drinking coffee. Once I spent an entire afternoon in my front yard, tying unpopped pieces

This silk charmeuse swatch was dyed after pushing marbles into the fabric and wrapping them with rubber bands. It was dyed in an acid dye bath.

Tools & Supplies

Scoured fabric

Various ties

Dye bath

Various objects (popcorn kernels, marbles, bottle caps, plastic bobbins, etc.)

Fabric marking pencil

of popcorn onto fabric and watching my children play. Really, once you've decided on your fabric, which ties you'll use, and in what pattern you'll tie them onto the fabric, all it takes is time. There are myriad ways to make bound-resist patterns, but let's discuss a few of the most common.

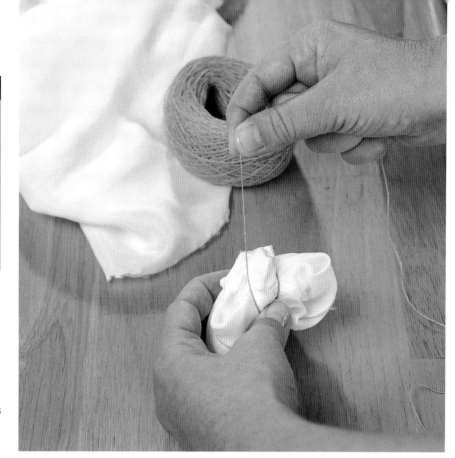

PHOTO 1. *Bundle the fabric before you wrap.*

Simple Bound Resists

Bound resists don't need to be fussy or complicated—all you need are ties and fabric. Here are some ideas to try.

You might first wrap a piece of fabric randomly with yarn, making sure the binding is tight, or you can wad up the fabric before you bind it (photo 1). An alternative is to gather the fabric together and bind it in several different places (photo 2), and yet another method is to use strips of fabric to bind other fabrics (photo 3). After binding, dye the fabric as desired.

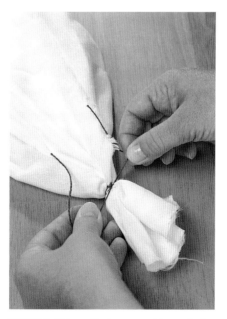

PHOTO 2. *This method was used to create the design in swatch 1 on page 72.*

PHOTO 3. *The green silk charmeuse fragment was used as a tie around a scarf made from a brown China silk blank. The bundle was then discharged in Thiox.*

Circular Patterns

Circular patterns are some of the most common in bound-resist shibori and definitely the most recognizable in tie-dyed T-shirts. To create this pattern, use your finger to push up an area of the cloth. Pinch the top of the cone you've made, and use yarn to wrap the cone from top to bottom (photo 4). As you make the wraps, manipulate the fabric so you don't have one area of cloth wrapping around an inner core. This ensures that a maximum amount of the fabric will be exposed to the dye, and you won't end up with large areas that aren't dyed.

When you've finished wrapping down the cone, wrap back up to the top and tightly tie the ends of the yarn together. Dye the fabric as desired.

PHOTO 5

Bound Objects

You can bind just about any small object to your fabric to make a pattern (photo 5), but I find that shapes tend to turn out very similarly—somewhere between a circle and a square—unless you bind the object very tightly. This is because of the way you gather the fabric at the base of the object. It may be tricky at first to hold onto the object and tie it in place tightly, but it will get easier with practice.

To create a specific pattern, you may wish to mark the fabric lightly with a fabric pencil to indicate the spot where you'd like the center of your resist to be (photo 6). This way, you can create any design you like

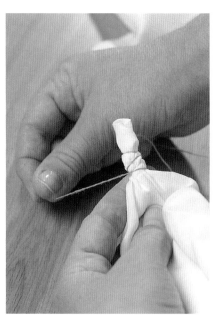

PHOTO 4

PHOTO 6

PHOTO 7

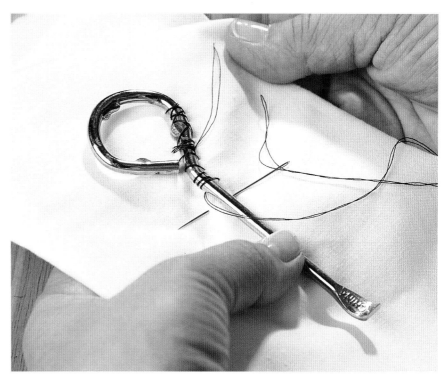

PHOTO 8

using bound-object resists. An all-over pattern is easily obtained this way.

To bind an object, push the fabric up with your finger to create a small cone (as you do with circular patterns, on page 70). Insert the object, gather the fabric around it, and pull the tie tight (photo 7). Use a square knot to tie off the object, making sure the fabric stays tight against the object as you secure it.

As with all these techniques, then dye the fabric as desired.

Recognizable Objects

You can also stitch items directly to the fabric, covering them with thread, and the result will be a subtle reproduction of the object. When you're stitching, go through all the fabric layers and tightly wrap the object with strong thread (photo 8).

Over-Dyeing

Every type of shibori can be dyed multiple times, but I find that over-dyeing in bound-resist shibori works particularly well because it's so easy to tie the resists tightly. Ties hold well for multiple dye baths, giving the cloth depth and character.

Look for examples of these variations of the bound-resist technique on pages 72–76.

Simple Bound Resists

Sample 1

The silk swatch you see in photo 1 was gathered and then tied in two places with cotton yarn before being dyed with fiber-reactive dye. The white cloth absorbed the dye so two very different shades were produced, giving the fabric an electric effect. This is a simple—but very illustrative—example of the techniques and the marks the resists make.

Samples 2a & 2b

A bound resist doesn't get much easier than this, as I just wadded up the silk fabric, randomly bound it with yarn, and dyed it with fiber-reactive dye. Note the similarity apparent in sample 2b, as this silk swatch was dyed in almost the identical manner.

Sample 3

The next swatch was folded in half and then bound with yarn in several places. I used a vat dye for this silk fabric.

Sample 4

I switched to sueded rayon for this swatch. This piece was bound with rubber bands and dyed with indigo.

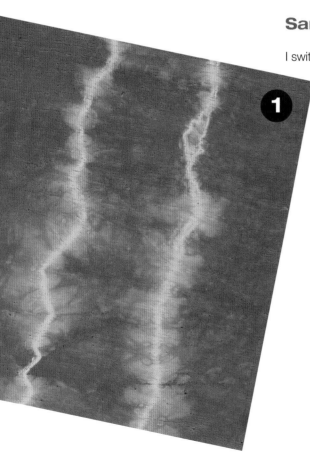

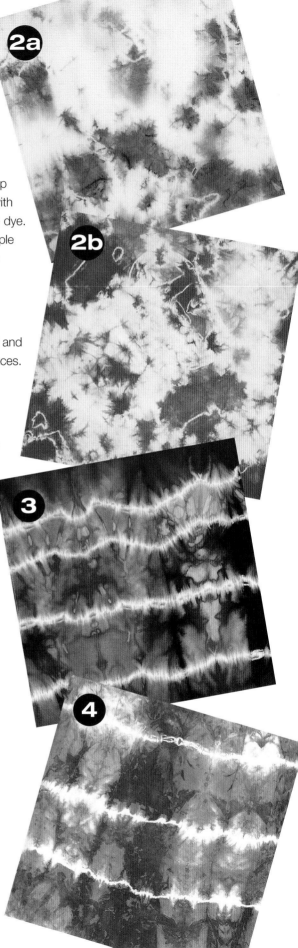

Circular Patterns

Sample 5

On this red sueded rayon, I tied several cones with cotton yarn and wrapped embroidery floss around them. In some places, I covered most of the cones to resist the Thiox. I like the way Thiox reacts with rayon, as it creates very definite patterns that you see in the photo.

Sample 6

In photo 6, this square China silk blank scarf was wrapped a lot near the top of the cone, creating the thicker band in the center. I used separate pieces of yarn to wrap it and make the "rings." It was dyed with acid dye.

Sample 7

Here's a completely different look. I used a light blue cotton fabric for this swatch and created several cones on the piece of fabric. I tied a very small-gauge string to get the "spider web" effect and dyed it with fiber-reactive dye.

Sample 8

This piece of cotton had to be re-dyed with indigo, as the initial tying resisted most of the dye by creating an inner core of fabric.

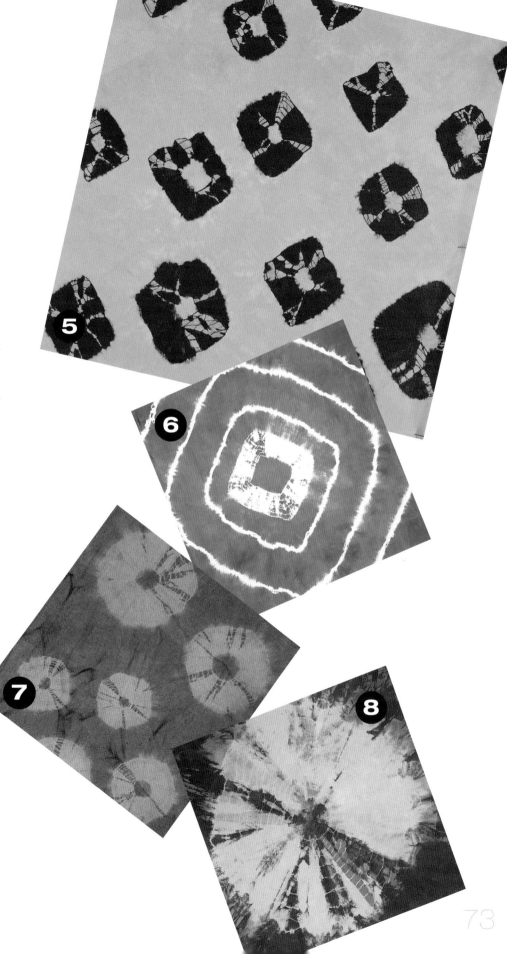

Bound Objects

Sample 9

The combination of tying the yarn very tightly around the cloth and using indigo made for a very bright and clear pattern, as you see in photo 9. The bound objects in this case were popcorn kernels, randomly pushed into the cloth to create cones when wrapped with cotton yarn. The white sueded rayon was dyed with indigo.

Sample 10

This odd swatch was made with silk dupioni. I pushed popcorn kernels into the fabric and then wrapped embroidery floss around them before dyeing the silk with fiber-reactive dye. I then spilled fabric paint on it—a happy accident that produced an intriguing piece of cloth.

Sample 11

There's another piece of interesting cloth in photo 11. This swatch was made from cotton print cloth that had already been dyed very lightly with an arashi pattern. I pushed marbles into the cloth and then wrapped rubber bands around the cones they created. After I prepared the resists, I dyed it with a vat dye.

Wrapping Objects

Sample 12

While looking around my studio for an object to bind, I ran across a church key and decided to wrap it with extra-strong thread, sewing the object through all the layers of cloth. The result left a subtle, yet recognizable, image on the silk georgette after it was dyed with acid dye.

This technique is similar to couching, a form of embroidery in which one object is stitched to the other. Look around to find objects that lend themselves to this kind of treatment, and you may be able to create some unique patterns in your shibori.

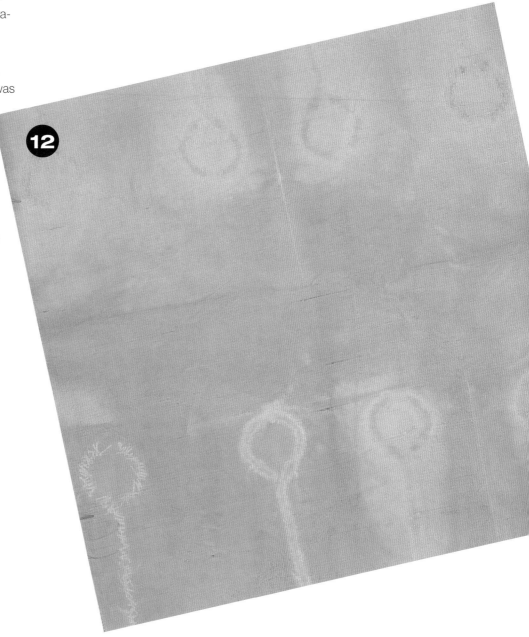

Over-Dyeing

Sample 13

I created the resist in the swatch you
see here by using marbles bound with
rubber bands. Then, the silk dupioni
was dyed gold in a fiber-reactive dye
bath. The process was repeated and
dyed turquoise. I initially thought the
result was a mistake. After it dried,
though, the colors were luminous on
the dupioni and it was most definitely
a keeper.

Sample 14

My next swatch began as yellow silk
dupioni. It was gathered and wrapped
with yarn, then dyed green with fiber-
reactive dye. I untied it and gathered it
again. I wrapped it with yarn, and finally
dyed it with turquoise vat dye.

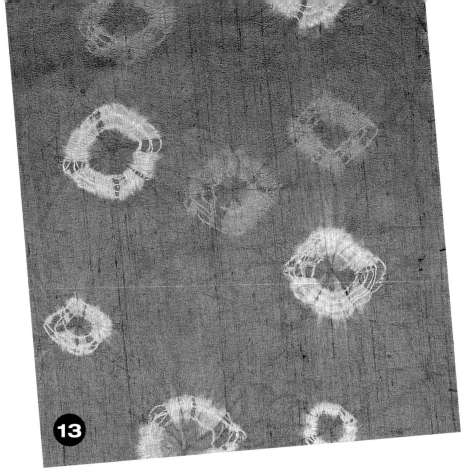

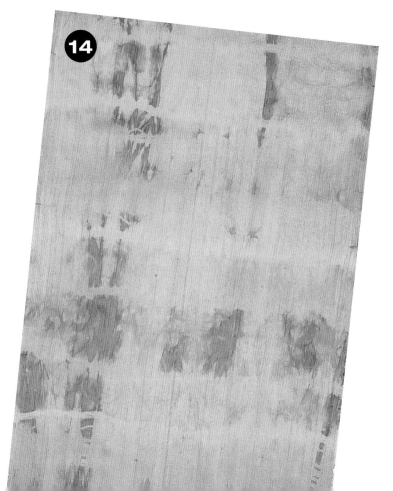

Envelope Pillows

The fabrics for these pillows were all dyed in the same dye baths. I started with two types of white fabric (a linen handkerchief material and a cotton print cloth) and dyed them tangerine before manipulating the fabric for shibori. To create a mottled appearance, I didn't stir the bath. I then bound the fabrics to resist dye penetration, and placed them in a raspberry dye bath.

Large Cotton Pillow

What You Do

Use a ½-inch (1.3 cm) seam allowance unless otherwise noted.

1 With scissors, cut a 60 x 26-inch (150 x 66 cm) piece of the pre-dyed cotton fabric.

2 Push a marble from the wrong side of the fabric to create a cone.

3 Use a rubber band to bind the marble tightly in place.

4 Repeat steps 2 and 3 to randomly place about 60 marbles all around the fabric.

5 Dye the fabric in the dye bath, following the instructions on page 25 for dyeing with fiber-reactive dyes. Rinse and let dry. Remove the marbles. Iron.

6 Fold the fabric in half along the long edge, right sides together, and press.

7 Pin the fabric together down the long edges. Stitch. There should now be three bound sides (two are stitched, and the other folded). One end should remain completely open.

8 Turn the cover right side out and place the pillow form inside. Fold the remaining edge over, as if wrapping a present, so that the fold looks like an envelope.

9 Hand sew a few carefully placed anchoring stitches, and then blanket stitch along the edge of the fold with embroidery floss to create a neat and finished appearance.

What You Need

Scissors

1 yard (.9 m) of white cotton print fabric, pre-dyed with tangerine fiber-reactive dye

Marbles

Rubber bands

Raspberry fiber-reactive dye bath

Iron

Chalk or water-soluble pencil

Measuring tape or ruler

Straight pins

Sewing machine

Sewing thread, raspberry

20 x 24-inch (51.6 x 61.9) pillow form

Small sewing needle

Embroidery floss, raspberry

What You Need

Scissors

1 yard (.9 m) of pink silk dupioni

1 yard (.9 m) of white cotton print fabric, pre-dyed with tangerine fiber-reactive dye

Marbles

Rubber bands

Popcorn kernels

Yarn

Raspberry fiber-reactive dye bath

Iron

Chalk or water-soluble pencil

Measuring tape or ruler

Straight pins

Sewing machine

Sewing thread, raspberry

20-inch (51.6 cm) square pillow form

Small sewing needle

Embroidery floss, raspberry

PILLOW Nº 2

Large Cotton Pillow with Pink Silk Backing

What You Do

Use a ½-inch (1.3 cm) seam allowance unless otherwise noted.

1 With scissors, cut a 22 x 22-inch (56.8 x 56.8 cm) piece of silk dupioni and set aside.

2 Cut a 22 x 22-inch (56.8 x 56.8 cm) square piece of the pre-dyed cotton fabric.

3 Push a marble from the wrong side of the fabric to the right side to create a cone with the fabric.

4 Use a rubber band to bind the marble tightly in place.

5 Repeat steps 2–4, randomly placing 10 to 20 marbles all around the fabric. Also bind the popcorn kernels, this time using yarn to secure them.

6 Dye the fabric in the dye bath, following the instructions on page 25 for dyeing with fiber-reactive dyes. Rinse and let dry. Iron.

7 Place the cotton and the silk with right sides together and press.

8 Pin the fabric together along three sides. Stitch. There should now be three stitched sides. One side should remain completely open.

9 Turn the cover right side out and place the pillow form inside. Fold the remaining edge over, as if wrapping a present, so that the fold looks like an envelope.

10 Hand sew a few carefully placed anchoring stitches, and then blanket stitch along the edge of the fold with embroidery floss to create a neat and finished appearance.

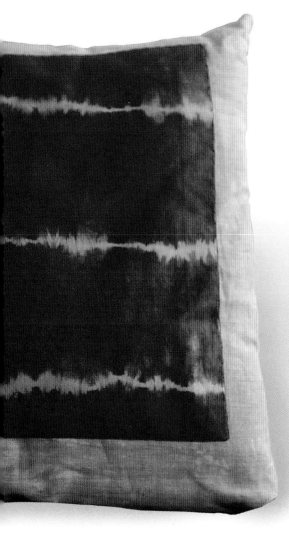

Orange Pillow with Appliqué

What You Do

Use a ½-inch (1.3 cm) seam allowance unless otherwise noted.

1 With scissors, cut a 16 x 15-inch (40.6 x 38.1 cm) piece of pre-dyed cotton fabric.

2 Fold the cloth and wrap it with string.

3 Dye the fabric in the dye bath, following the instructions on page 25 for dyeing with fiber-reactive dyes, and then rinse. Let dry.

4 Turn under 1 inch (2.5 cm) on each edge and press.

5 Cut a 40 x 18-inch (101.6 x 45.7 cm) piece of the pre-dyed linen fabric.

6 Fold the fabric in half along the long edge, right sides together, and press.

7 Pin the fabric together down the long edges. Stitch. There should now be three bound sides (two are stitched, and the other folded). One end should remain completely open.

8 Turn the cover right side out and place the pillow form inside.

9 Center and pin the piece of shibori you made in steps 1 through 4 to the pillow cover. Use embroidery floss to blanket stitch it in place.

10 Fold the remaining edge over, as if wrapping a present, so that the fold looks like an envelope.

11 Hand sew a few carefully placed anchoring stitches, and then blanket stitch along the edge of the fold with embroidery floss to create a neat and finished appearance.

What You Need

Scissors

1 yard (.9 m) of white cotton print fabric, pre-dyed with tangerine fiber-reactive dye

Cotton string

Raspberry fiber-reactive dye bath

Iron

1 yard (.9 m) of white linen handkerchief fabric, pre-dyed with tangerine fiber-reactive dye

Chalk or water-soluble pencil

Measuring tape or ruler

Straight pins

Sewing machine

Sewing thread, tangerine

18-inch square (46.4 cm) pillow form

Small sewing needle

Embroidery floss, tangerine and raspberry

Fringe Pillow

What You Do

Use a ½-inch (1.3 cm) seam allowance unless otherwise noted.

1 With scissors, cut a 15 x 19-inch (38.1 x 49 cm) piece of silk dupioni and set aside.

2 Cut a 16 x 18-inch (41.3 x 45.7 cm) piece of pre-dyed cotton fabric.

3 Push up the cotton fabric from the wrong side to the right side to make a cone in the fabric. Use thread to wrap around the cone so that it will resist the dye.

4 Dye the fabric in the dye bath, following the instructions on page 25 for dyeing with fiber-reactive dyes. Rinse and let dry.

5 Place the silk and cotton together with right sides facing. Align one long edge of the silk with one long edge of the cotton; the cotton piece should be more-or-less centered along the silk's edge. Pin in place. Stitch.

6 Turn the pillow cover so the wrong sides are together. Fold one short side of the silk over the short side of the cotton. The wrong side of the silk will touch the right side of the cotton. There will be a 1¾-inch (4.4 cm) overlap. Press. Repeat for the other short side.

7 Measure and cut a length of fusible web tape that will run down one short side of the cotton. Place the web right at the cotton's edge, overlap the silk, and press to fuse, following the manufacturer's instructions. Repeat for the other side. Three edges of the pillow cover should now be closed, and one completely open.

8 Place the pillow form inside the cover. Fold the remaining edge over, as if wrapping a present, so that the fold looks like an envelope.

9 Sew a few carefully placed anchoring stitches, and then blanket stitch along the edge of the fold with embroidery floss to create a neat and finished appearance.

10 As a finishing touch, clip the loose part of the silk overlaps (created in step 7) every ½ inch (1.3 cm) to create fringe. Press the fringe to the outside.

What You Need

Scissors

1 yard (.9 m) of pink silk dupioni

1 yard (.9 m) of white cotton print fabric, pre-dyed with tangerine fiber-reactive dye

Cotton thread

Raspberry fiber-reactive dye bath

Straight pins

Sewing machine

Sewing thread, raspberry

Iron

Measuring tape or ruler

Fusible web tape

14 x 16-inch (36.1 x 41.3 cm) pillow form

Small sewing needle

Embroidery floss, raspberry

Bound-Resist T-Shirts

I am always in search of the perfect T-shirt. Because these had small stains, they were pulled from my closet for a new look. One great thing about a T-shirt is that it can always be dyed.

Blue T-Shirt with Bound Resist

What You Do

1 Bunch the T-shirt from side to side and bind a rubber band around the body of the shirt. Do the same with the sleeves and the neck.

2 Dye the T-shirt in the indigo dye bath, following the instructions on page 29.

3 Rinse the T-shirt (with the rubber bands in place) until the water runs clear. Remove the rubber bands and let dry before ironing, or you may choose to remove the rubber bands after the T-shirt has dried.

What You Need

Cotton T-shirt

Rubber bands

Indigo dye bath

Iron

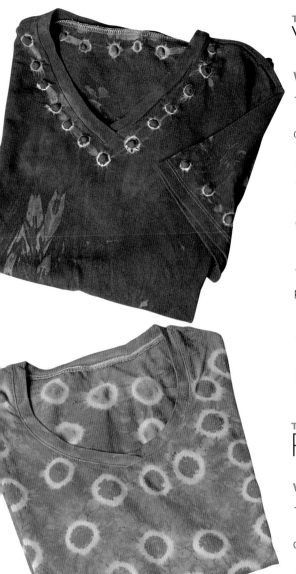

V-Neck with Popcorn Resist

What You Do

1 Push a kernel of popcorn from the inside of the shirt to the outside to create a cone with the fabric.

2 Use the yarn to bind the kernel tightly in place.

3 Repeat steps 1 and 2 to add kernels around the edge of the shirt.

4 Dye the T-shirt in the indigo dye bath, following the directions on page 29.

5 Rinse the T-shirt (with the kernels in place) until the water runs clear.

6 Leave the resists tied while the T-shirt dries.

What You Need

Unpopped popcorn kernels

Cotton T-shirt

Small-gauge yarn (for ties)

Indigo dye bath

Blue fabric paint

Small paintbrush

7 Use fabric paint and a paintbrush to paint over the areas of the T-shirt where the kernels protrude. Let dry.

8 Remove the resists and kernels. Do not iron.

Pink T-Shirt with Marble Resist

What You Do

1 Push a marble from the inside of the shirt to the outside to create a cone with the fabric.

2 Use rubber bands to bind the marbles tightly in place.

3 Repeat steps 1 and 2 until all the resists are in place.

4 Dye the T-shirt in the purple fiber-reactive dye bath, following the instructions on page 25.

5 Rinse the T-shirt (with the marbles in place) until the water runs clear.

What You Need

Marbles

Cotton T-shirt

Rubber bands

Purple fiber-reactive dye bath

Iron

6 Remove the rubber bands and marbles while the shirt is still wet. Allow to dry before ironing.

Tip

The T-shirts used for these projects are all 95 percent cotton and 5 percent spandex. They dyed evenly and without difficulty. Of course, 100 percent cotton T-shirts will work equally well, if not better.

Stitching and Gathering

Although stitching and gathering cloth is an ancient form of shibori in Japan, the Javanese word *tritik* is commonly used to describe the process. In this form of resist dyeing, cloth is stitched and then pulled or gathered into tight bundles before being placed in the dye bath. The resulting patterns are highly controlled and tend to be more orderly in appearance than other forms of shibori.

*Swatch
of silk dupioni that
was dyed with acid dye. Read
more about this swatch on page 90.*

Often, the pieces created with this process retain tiny holes from the stitching process, thus adding further visual interest to the designs.

One of my favorite things about tritik is that it's a terrifically mobile process. It's easier to transport than knitting, and equally addictive. Also, the designs you create with tritik can vary greatly, from abstract, to pictorial, to geometric. Cotton and most silks are the easiest fabrics to work with when doing tritik. I particularly like to work with silk dupioni. Although it's by no means impossible to work with silk charmeuse or China silk, I find that the hand of those fabrics makes them harder to control.

I recommend using quilting thread for this type of shibori, but you can use any type of thread that's strong enough to be tied yet not so thick that it leaves large holes in the fabric. If the fabric is the type that's not easily torn, it's best to double the thread. Also, use the smallest needle you are comfortable working with. This gives you more control over your design.

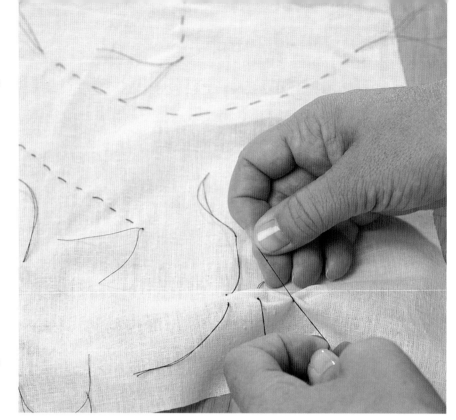

PHOTO 1

What You Need

Fabric

Sewing needles

Colorful threads in different weights

Sharp scissors

Iron

Fabric marking pencil

Various templates for designs (to make circles, squares, etc.)

Sewing machine (optional)

Running Stitch

Traditionally, only two hand stitches are used for tritik. The most common is the basic running stitch, which works very well for detailed designs. The running stitch is made by weaving the needle in and out of the fabric at regular intervals. When you use a running stitch, you'll need to decide how far apart you'd like each stitch to be. The farther apart the stitches, the less detail your design will have. Always leave at least a 3-inch (7.5 cm) thread tail at each end of the stitching so that you can easily pull it to gather the fabric and ready it for dyeing (photo 1).

I recommend doing a few samples of running stitches before committing to a large project; see the random examples in photo 1. Take lots of small pieces of cloth and try any com-bination you can think of—stitches on the diagonal, small stitches, large stitches, random stitches across the width of the fabric, etc. You can also repeat your pattern with another gauge of thread and you'll have completely different results from your initial stitching. After you've finished gathering the fabric, dye it as desired.

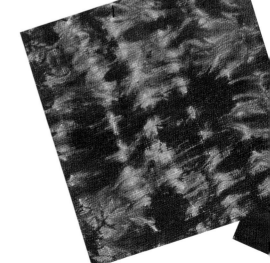

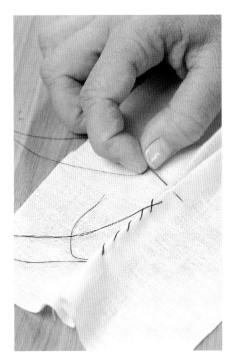

PHOTO 2

Whipstitch

Whipstitch is the second type of stitch used for tritik. A slanted stitch where the needle is inserted perpendicular to the fabric edge, whipstitch works well for creating a chevron pattern in the cloth, but it's not quite as easy to work as running stitch. When doing whipstitch, it helps to fold the cloth and iron it before you begin, although this step is not absolutely necessary (photo 2).

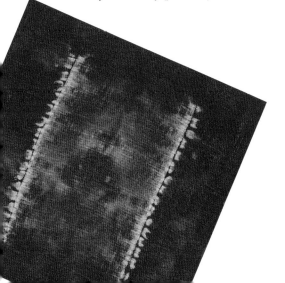

Mokume

Mokume is the Japanese term for wood grain and describes a particular richly textured shibori design. This pattern is created by using running stitches in parallel lines across a piece of fabric. To create mokume, knot the thread at one end before you begin. Make lines of small running stitches that are fairly close together and vary slightly in length. To finish, use one of these methods: gather and knot the thread with an overhand knot, or tie the thread ends of one side of the stitching with the ends from the other side, using square knots. If you use the latter method, the finished piece can be quite different, as less dye will seep into the cloth because the tie will be much tighter.

The mokume technique is illustrated on page 92.

PHOTO 3

Gathering and Then Stitching

In the bound-resists section of this book (page 68), I discussed using different ties to bind fabric before dyeing. Each tie, while different, will create a similar look. A variant of that bound-resist look is to gather the fabric and then stitch it into place.

Use your finger to push up an area of the cloth and pinch the top of the cone you've made. Pass the needle and thread back and forth through the gathered cloth several times (photo 3). Tie the thread ends together tightly.

PHOTO 6

Folding and Then Stitching

Using stitches to hold fabric folds makes it easy to create geometric patterns on your shibori cloth. When you use this method, however, keep in mind that interior folds absorb less dye than exterior folds do. The variations of folding and then stitching the fabric (photos 4 and 5) are endless. After folding, you may want to iron the cloth to maintain its shape.

Drawing on Fabric

For this method, imagine your needle and thread as just another type of pencil. You can "draw" anything you like on the fabric using running stitches (photo 6), and then dye the design into the cloth.

Use a washable fabric marking pencil to draw your design onto the fabric. You can use templates, if you wish. Note: I've made the mistake of using a regular pencil on silk—it never came out.

Follow the marked design by making small, evenly spaced running stitches. Begin a new thread whenever you begin a new design element. Pull the threads tightly to gather the fabric and tie the ends into a square knot. Dye the fabric as desired.

PHOTOS 4 AND 5. *Any combination of folds and stitches can be used in this variation of shibori. Pull tightly to gather the stitches and knot securely. Remember to leave a tail to knot the thread.*

PHOTO 7

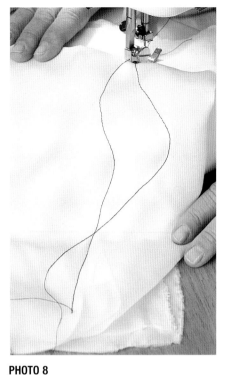

PHOTO 8

PHOTO 9

Machine-Stitched Shibori

For the person well acquainted with a sewing machine, this contemporary form of stitched shibori will be of great interest. It's an exciting form of mark making. By setting the machine for long basting stitches and a loose bobbin tension for gathering, it's quick and easy to make multiple lines and other designs (photos 7, 8, and 9). Although the initial stitching is almost immediate, keep in mind that removing the stitches can sometimes take awhile.

There are alternative ways to create machine-stitched shibori. Some of my favorite pieces involve sewing layers of fabric together with very tight, short stitches, but not gathering the stitches before dyeing the fabric. The result is an image that's only subtly apparent.

Look for many examples of stitched-and-gathered shibori on pages 90–99. You'll also find illustrations for several of the stitches.

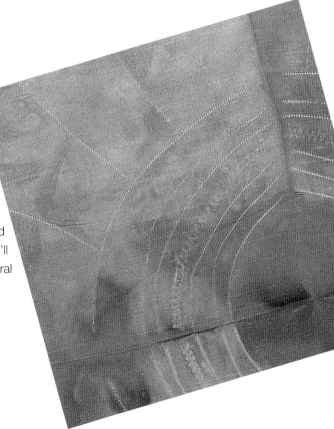

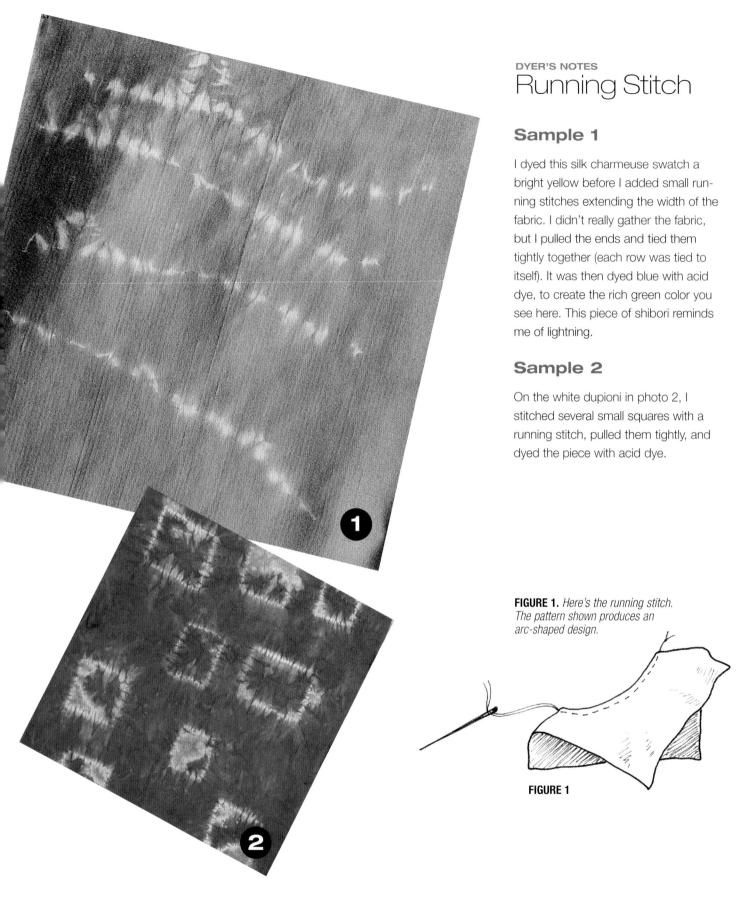

Running Stitch

Sample 1

I dyed this silk charmeuse swatch a bright yellow before I added small running stitches extending the width of the fabric. I didn't really gather the fabric, but I pulled the ends and tied them tightly together (each row was tied to itself). It was then dyed blue with acid dye, to create the rich green color you see here. This piece of shibori reminds me of lightning.

Sample 2

On the white dupioni in photo 2, I stitched several small squares with a running stitch, pulled them tightly, and dyed the piece with acid dye.

FIGURE 1. *Here's the running stitch. The pattern shown produces an arc-shaped design.*

FIGURE 1

Whipstitch

Sample 3

Before stitching this swatch, I folded the fabric with a small trench between the two areas that were whipstitched together. (You can see this kind of fold in photo 2 on page 87.) This stitching forms a chevron pattern on the finished piece. I deliberately didn't agitate the fabric in the Thiox discharge bath, so I got uneven results. This silk dupioni was originally green.

Sample 4

I used hemp for this piece. I used both running stitches and whipstitches to form the pattern: the lines in the middle of the fabric were made by pinching the fabric together into a fold, sewing it with a whipstitch, gathering the fabric, and tightly tying the ends together. The line at the top was made by pinching a fold of fabric and sewing it with a running stitch, gathering the fabric, and tightly tying the ends together. This addition of the pinched fabric doubles the pattern you would ordinarily see and by doing so creates an entirely new design. This piece was dyed with a vat dye.

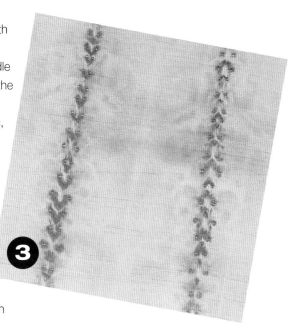

FIGURES 2 AND 3. *A pattern of chevron stripes is created by inserting the needle from the back of the fold. Let the stitches build up on the needle until they are pushed off.*

FIGURE 2

FIGURE 3

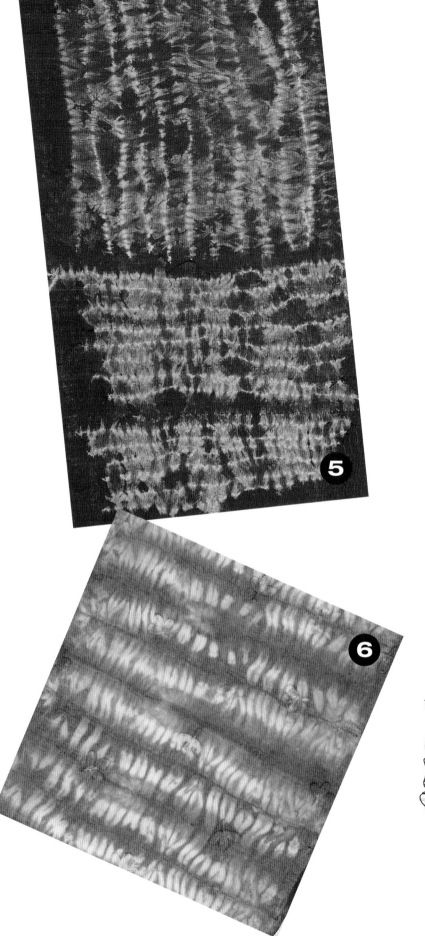

5

Mokume

Sample 5

I used the mokume technique on two sections of this swatch in photo 5, stitching each section in a different direction. This piece was the prototype for the pashmina project on page 107, but the linen in this swatch created a much more defined pattern than the more loosely woven fabric in the pashmina. I used the overhand method of knotting the thread ends. This piece was dyed with acid dye.

Sample 6

For the swatch in photo 6, however, I used the other technique of knotting—end-to-end with square knots. This embroidered cotton was folded with an accordion fold, stitched with running stitches, tied, and then dyed with fiber-reactive dye.

6

FIGURE 4. *Use lines of running stitches to mimic wood grain, the inspiration for mokume.*

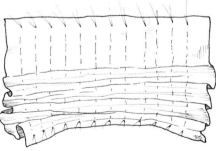

FIGURE 4

Gathering and Stitching

Sample 7

Here you see silk organza that was dyed with acid dye; it was gathered into a cone and stitched, as in photo 3 on page 87. At the end of an evening in the studio, I came across this small piece of fabric and decided to spend five extra minutes working on it before bed. It looked great in the morning! So many successes in shibori arise from spontaneity and intuition.

Notice the detail you can see in this swatch—the lines of stitching are still apparent in the finished piece of shibori. Stitching can add depth and visual interest to your work.

Folding and Stitching

Sample 8

I folded this silk scarf into a cone, and then stitched it in two places to create the inner and outer circles. However, the small circles you see on the perimeter were a complete surprise. The variations of folding, stitching, and gathering are almost endless, as you'll see in the swatches that follow.

Sample 9

In photo 9, this piece of silk dupioni was folded in half, then in half again to form a square. I ironed the fabric and tightly sewed the edges together with whipstitches. It was dyed in an acid dye bath.

Sample 10

The linen piece in photo 10 was accordion-folded and ironed in place, but I used a running stitch for this swatch. I stitched along the edge of each fold before tying the ends and dyeing it with vat dye.

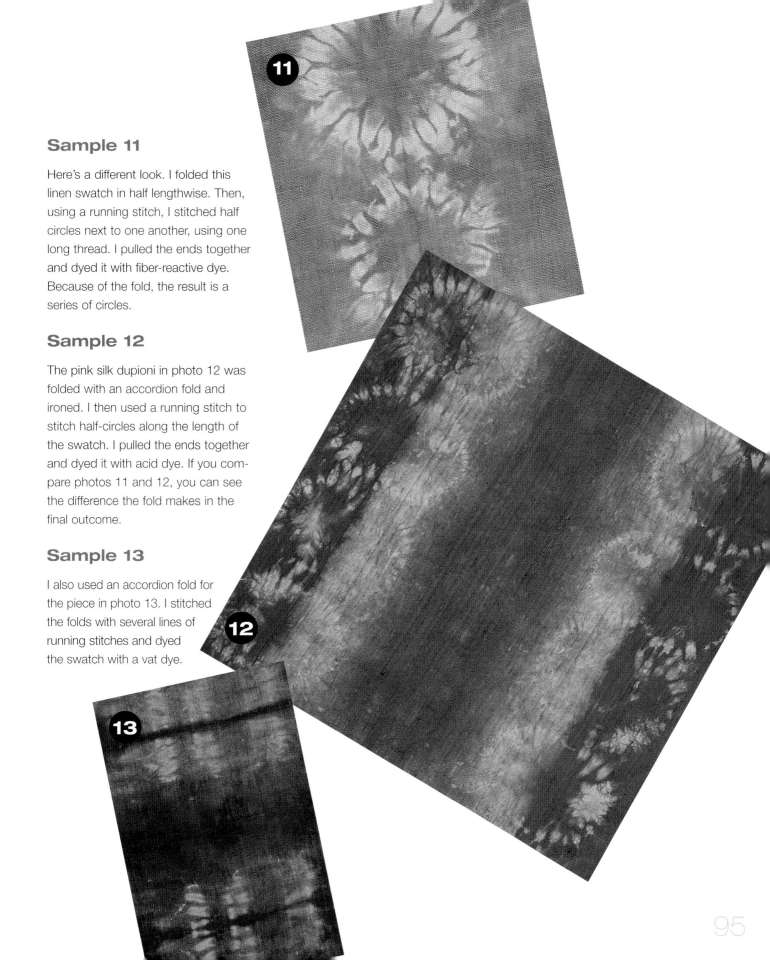

Sample 11

Here's a different look. I folded this linen swatch in half lengthwise. Then, using a running stitch, I stitched half circles next to one another, using one long thread. I pulled the ends together and dyed it with fiber-reactive dye. Because of the fold, the result is a series of circles.

Sample 12

The pink silk dupioni in photo 12 was folded with an accordion fold and ironed. I then used a running stitch to stitch half-circles along the length of the swatch. I pulled the ends together and dyed it with acid dye. If you compare photos 11 and 12, you can see the difference the fold makes in the final outcome.

Sample 13

I also used an accordion fold for the piece in photo 13. I stitched the folds with several lines of running stitches and dyed the swatch with a vat dye.

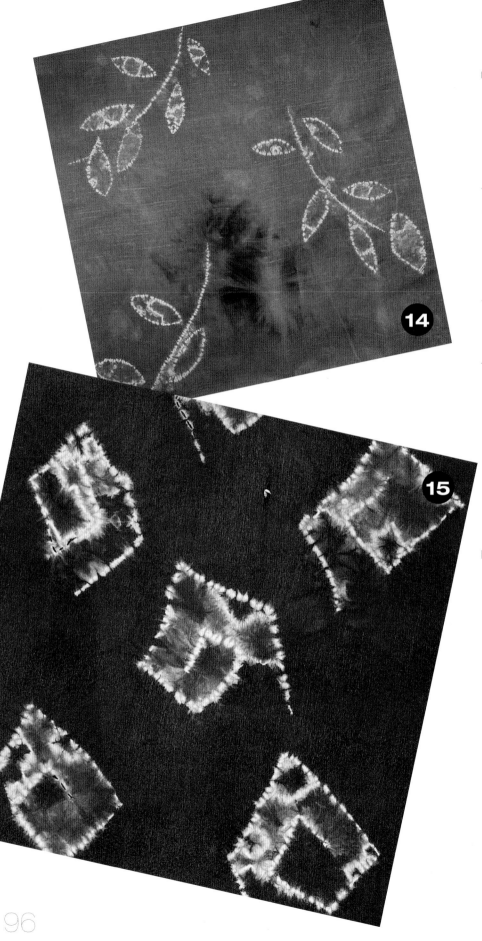

Drawing on Fabric

Sample 14

I drew the design on the silk charmeuse first, and then stitched each leaf with a separate piece of thread before gathering it tightly. An image of leaves is something I often draw or paint, and I enjoyed transferring it to cloth and "drawing" it with thread. This swatch was dyed in acid dye.

Sample 15

The pattern created in photo 15 is less literal and more geometric. I simply stitched a design on the China silk, gathered it, and dyed it with vat dye.

FIGURE 5. *Use the needle to "draw" on the fabric.*

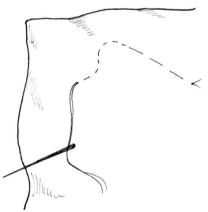

FIGURE 5

Machine-Stitched Shibori

Sample 16

You can create lots of varied pieces with machine stitching. Stitching a piece in this manner is amazingly quick and easy. In photo 16, this silk dupioni swatch was stitched lengthwise first, and then turned and stitched across part of the width. After it was gathered, it was submerged in an acid dye bath. I loved seeing the way the dye was absorbed less evenly when the cloth was stitched in two directions.

Samples 17a & 17b

In photo 17a, see the undulating patterns that resulted from carefree lines of stitching. This green sueded rayon was folded in half, stitched and gathered, and then dyed with a vat dye. Compare this to photo 17b, where the lines of stitching are straighter; this swatch was made from silk charmeuse and was not folded before it was stitched and dyed in an acid dye bath.

Samples 18a & 18b

In 18a, a piece of cotton was stitched in lines similar to mokume before it was gathered and dyed with vat dye. In photo 18b, you see a much looser pattern, created on linen with wavy stitching lines and vat dye.

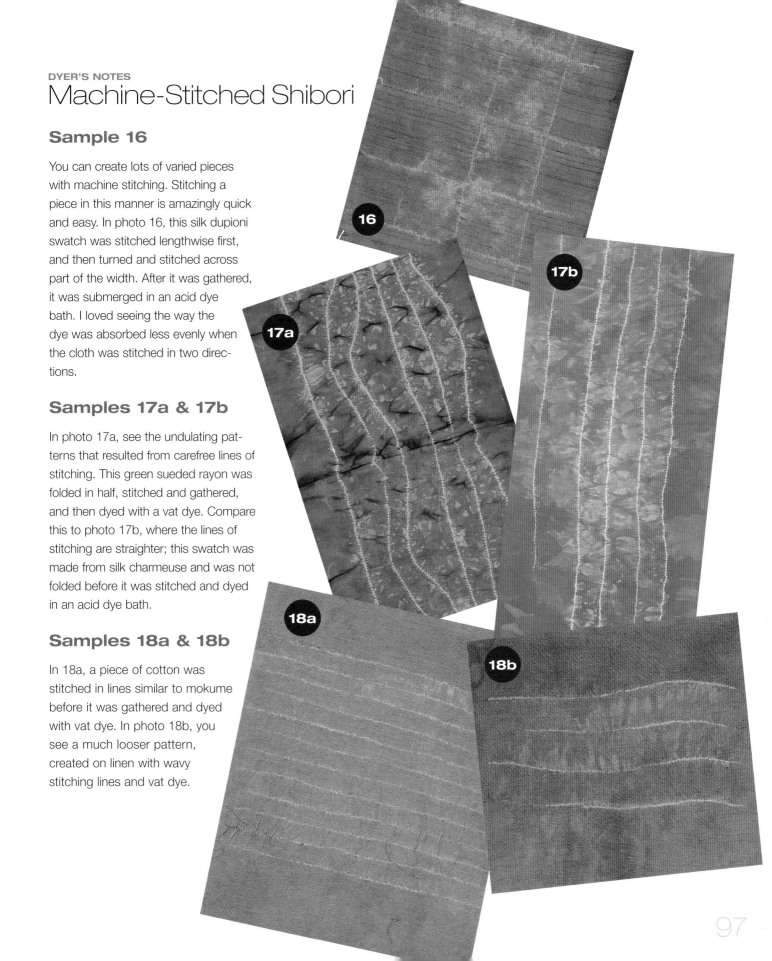

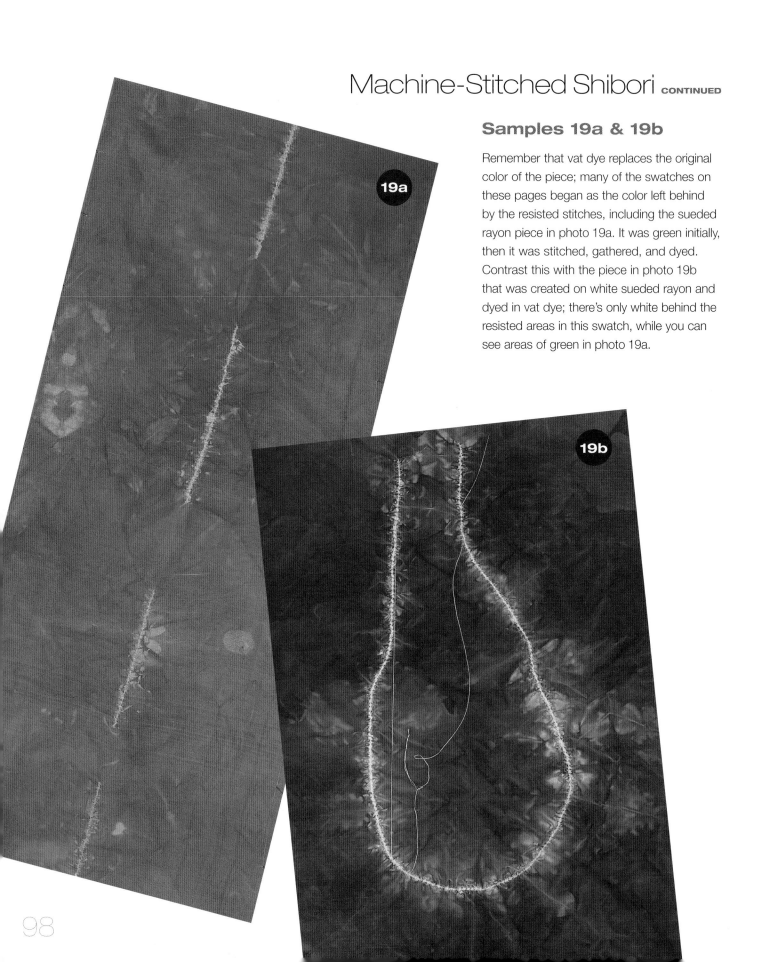

Machine-Stitched Shibori

Samples 19a & 19b

Remember that vat dye replaces the original color of the piece; many of the swatches on these pages began as the color left behind by the resisted stitches, including the sueded rayon piece in photo 19a. It was green initially, then it was stitched, gathered, and dyed. Contrast this with the piece in photo 19b that was created on white sueded rayon and dyed in vat dye; there's only white behind the resisted areas in this swatch, while you can see areas of green in photo 19a.

Samples 20a & 20b

The last two swatches illustrate a different technique you can use, that is, stitching without gathering. The piece in photo 20a is made with silk charmeuse that was folded into a cone shape, stitched, and dyed with acid dye; the swatch in photo 20b was folded into a square and decorated with a diamond pattern of stitching, along with a straight line of stitching around the edge. Rayon that was originally green, it was dyed in vat dye. To reiterate, neither of these pieces was gathered.

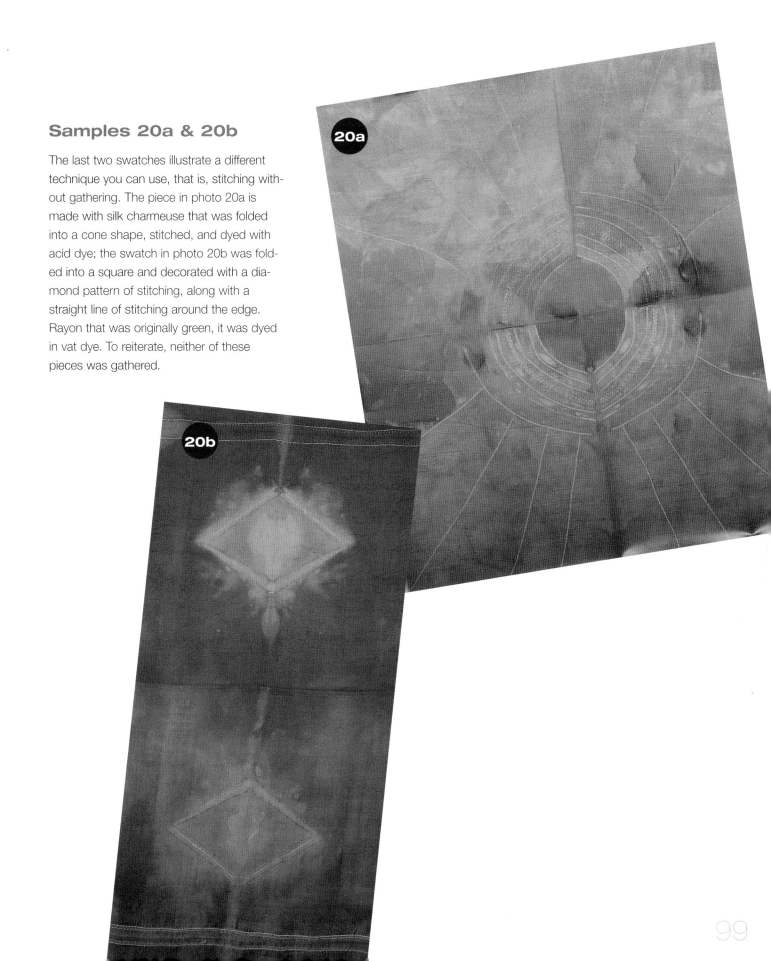

Decorative Borders for Pants

The decorative borders on these pairs of pants were created from shibori samples I made for the stitching and gathering chapter in this book.

What You Do

1 Make shibori samples using the fabric, needles, thread, and various stitching and gathering techniques. For this project, I used linen for the blue jeans and silk charmeuse for the silk pants.

2 Dye the fabric in the dye bath. For the linen I used fiber-reactive dyes (page 25); for the silk, acid dyes (page 27).

3 Fold the fabric so it's all the same width and the rough edges are tucked under. Pin the fabric to the bottom of the pants and sew in place. You can use lightweight silk yarn to sew your fabric the way I did with the blue jeans—the running stitch becomes part of the design. If you are working with

What You Need

Fabric, about ¼ yard (58.1 cm) each of silk and linen

Sewing needles

Sewing thread or lightweight yarn to match the shibori

Green fiber-reactive dye bath (for linen); green acid dye bath (for silk)

Straight pins

Pants

Glass beads (optional)

lightweight fabric, use a light thread and a tiny needle to leave no obvious mark on the cloth.

4 Add a beaded embellishment, if desired.

Machine-Stitched Shibori Quilt

This bright, inventive quilt, called *House It Going?*, was designed and made by Marguerite Gignoux. She used a wide variety of embellishment techniques to accent the many small swatches of shibori used to make the houses. This is a nice project to do once you've gathered a large assortment of left-over shibori cloth.

What You Do

1 Make the background by first using scissors to cut long lengths of the yellow cloth, each on a slight diagonal. Use the sewing machine and yellow thread to stitch different lengths of cloth together so that the different hues combine in a whimsical repeat, combining the pieces to equal at least 24 x 36 (61.9 x 92.9) inches. Press all the seams open with an iron. With a sewing needle and thread, loosely topstitch the pieced background onto the cotton batting. Cut the pieced background into the shape you want the final quilt to be.

2 From the shibori cloth, cut whimsically shaped squares, rectangles, and triangles in various sizes to make the houses, roofs, doors, and windows.

3 Use the sewing machine and red thread to stitch the shibori pieces directly to the quilted yellow background. Use straight stitch, triple stitch, and satin stitch. If desired, add small bits of batting to puff up each shape.

4 Use the beading needle and beading thread to embellish the houses with beads. Decorate the edges of roofs, doors, and windows.

5 Once all of the houses and embellishments are complete, use the sewing machine and yellow thread to add decorative stitching. This quilt features outlines of houses.

What You Need

Scissors

Six ½-yard (5.9 m) lengths of muslin and/or print cotton that have been dyed in different concentrations of yellow fiber-reactive dye baths

Sewing machine

Sewing thread, yellow and red

Iron

Sewing needle

1 yard (.9 m) of cotton batting

Assortment of shibori cloth swatches (linen, silk organza, cotton print cloth, and ramie dyed in fiber-reactive dyes)

Beading needle

Beading thread

Variety of small beads (cubes, bugle beads, seed beads, sequins, etc.)

Paper-backed fusible web

3 yards (2.7 m) of variegated satin cording

Finished dimensions: approximately 18 x 36 inches (46.4 x 92.9 cm)

6 Use the sewing machine and red thread to zigzag stitch around the entire work.

7 Create a backing for the quilt by piecing together leftover shibori samples. The final stitched backing should be larger than the front of the quilt.

8 Following the manufacturer's instructions, use the fusible web to join the front and back of the quilt (wrong sides together). The backing should extend beyond the finished work.

9 Use the sewing machine and red thread to zigzag stitch the edges of the quilt. Trim off any excess backing fabric.

10 Use the sewing machine and red thread to zigzag stitch the satin cording to the edges of the quilt. The cording should butt up right to the edge of the quilt.

Tip

Machine-stitched shibori was used quite a bit in this project. Here are some ideas for making your own pieces: accordion-fold the cloth and baste it; make triangular folds in the fabric and baste it; baste the fabric in parallel strips and pull the threads to gather the cloth; or make curved parallel lines and circular patterns.

Machine-Stitched Table Runner

Making a table runner is another easy project; if you can sew a straight seam, you can create something funky *and* elegant for your dining room.

What You Need

Scissors

Pieces of heavy linen that total about 19 x 100 inches (48.3 x 254 cm)

Sewing machine

Sewing thread, green and blue

Green vat dye bath

Indigo dye bath

Iron

Straight pins

Cotton sailcloth, about 19 x 92 inches (48.3 x 233.7 cm)

Sewing needle

Finished dimensions: approximately 18 x 90 inches (45 x 225 cm)

What You Do

1 With scissors, cut four 19 x 18-inch (48.3 x 45.7 cm) rectangles and two 19 x 11-inch (48.3 x 27.9 cm) rectangles from the heavy linen fabric.

2 Use the sewing machine and thread to stitch several straight lines on each fabric piece. Pull each of the thread ends taut to gather the fabric. Tie the thread ends together to secure the gather.

3 Dye the large pieces in the green vat dye bath (page 31) and the small pieces in the indigo dye bath (page 29). Rinse the fabric until the water runs clear and iron to dry.

4 Place two green squares together with right sides facing, but the patterns going in opposite directions. Carefully pin the squares together. Stitch along one edge, using a narrow seam allowance. Press the seam allowance

flat. Continue piecing and sewing the squares together to make a long strip. Add one blue square to each end of the strip.

5 Turn the pieced strip face down on the sailcloth and pin the two fabrics together, letting each blue end extend evenly past the end of the sailcloth. Use the sewing machine and thread to stitch the fabrics together along each side, using a narrow side allowance.

6 Turn the table runner right side out and iron it flat.

7 Fold the blue fabric over the end of the runner, as if wrapping a present, so that the fold looks like an envelope. Pin the fabric in place and sew it down by hand with a neat hemstitch. Repeat for the other end of the runner.

Tip

How big is a table runner? As far as I know, there aren't rules about how small or large a table runner should be. For this one, I measured the width and length of my dining room table and decided the runner should take up one-third of the width of the table and hang over the edges by about 6 inches (15.2 cm). When you make your own, determine the amount of fabric you'll need by measuring your table and deciding how you'd like the runner to look.

Stitched Rayon Wrap

While shopping at a fabric store, I was thrilled to find the white,
undyed rayon pashmina that serves as the base for this project.
You should never underestimate a fantastic blank.

What You Need

Rayon wrap

Tapestry needle

Lightweight yarn

Red fiber-reactive dye bath

What You Do

1 Working perpendicularly across and to each end of the wrap, sew approximately 2 inches (5.1 cm) of running stitches at regular intervals, using the tapestry needle and yarn.

2 Working from the selvages, sew running stitches in blocks to approximately halfway across the fabric. After completing a block in one direction, move to the other end of the wrap and complete another block from that end in the same direction. Turn the fabric around and create a block from the opposite direction. Again, move to the other end of the cloth and repeat.

The reason for jumping back and forth from one end of the fabric to the other is that you will be able to finish with an obvious middle block. This middle block may be wider or narrower than the others, but it will complete an obvious pattern without too much measuring.

3 Pull the stitches and tie them tightly with the lightweight yarn.

4 Dye the fabric in the dye bath, following the instructions on page 25 for dyeing with fiber-reactive dyes.

5 Rinse the fabric until the water runs clear. You can either untie the yarn at this point or wait until the cloth is dry.

Tip

Because the weave of this ready-made pashmina is not extremely tight and wouldn't show needle holes, I opted for a tapestry needle and lightweight yarn to make the stitches. The yarn and thread also allowed me to make the patterns large. For more tightly woven fabrics, use a thin needle and a light sewing thread.

Multiple
Techniques

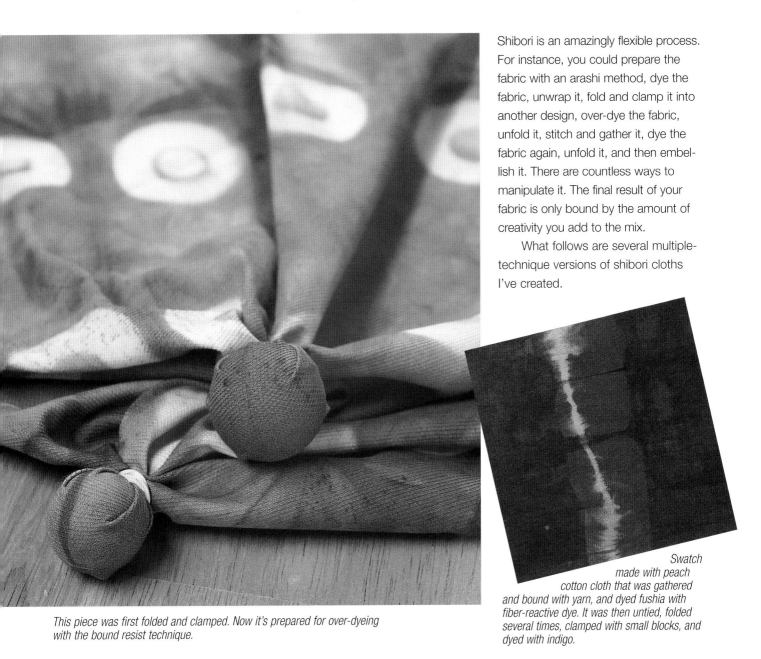

Shibori is an amazingly flexible process. For instance, you could prepare the fabric with an arashi method, dye the fabric, unwrap it, fold and clamp it into another design, over-dye the fabric, unfold it, stitch and gather it, dye the fabric again, unfold it, and then embellish it. There are countless ways to manipulate it. The final result of your fabric is only bound by the amount of creativity you add to the mix.

What follows are several multiple-technique versions of shibori cloths I've created.

This piece was first folded and clamped. Now it's prepared for over-dyeing with the bound resist technique.

Swatch made with peach cotton cloth that was gathered and bound with yarn, and dyed fushia with fiber-reactive dye. It was then untied, folded several times, clamped with small blocks, and dyed with indigo.

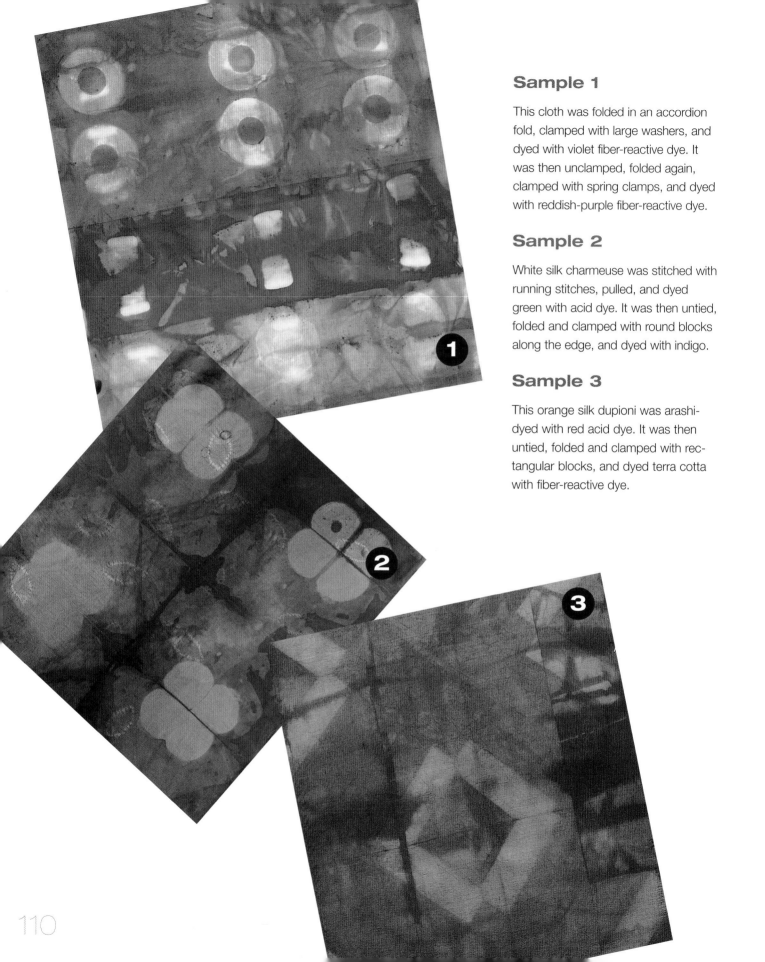

Sample 1

This cloth was folded in an accordion fold, clamped with large washers, and dyed with violet fiber-reactive dye. It was then unclamped, folded again, clamped with spring clamps, and dyed with reddish-purple fiber-reactive dye.

Sample 2

White silk charmeuse was stitched with running stitches, pulled, and dyed green with acid dye. It was then untied, folded and clamped with round blocks along the edge, and dyed with indigo.

Sample 3

This orange silk dupioni was arashi-dyed with red acid dye. It was then untied, folded and clamped with rectangular blocks, and dyed terra cotta with fiber-reactive dye.

Sample 4

This swatch was made with white China silk that was folded, stitched, and dyed with electric blue fiber-reactive dye. It was then untied and arashi-dyed with midnight blue fiber-reactive dye.

Sample 5

Made from pale green cotton cloth that was bound with a circular binding technique, this swatch was dyed with blue fiber-reactive dye. It was then unbound, stitched with concentric circles using running stitch, pulled tightly, and dyed with indigo.

Sample 6

Pale pink linen was stitched and gathered with running stitches and dyed pale green. It was then stitched and gathered again with running stitch and dyed with indigo.

Sample 7

This pale yellow cotton was folded and stitched with running stitches and whipstitches (some pulled, some not pulled) and dyed with gold fiber-reactive dye. The remaining stitches were then gathered, and it was dyed with green fiber-reactive dye.

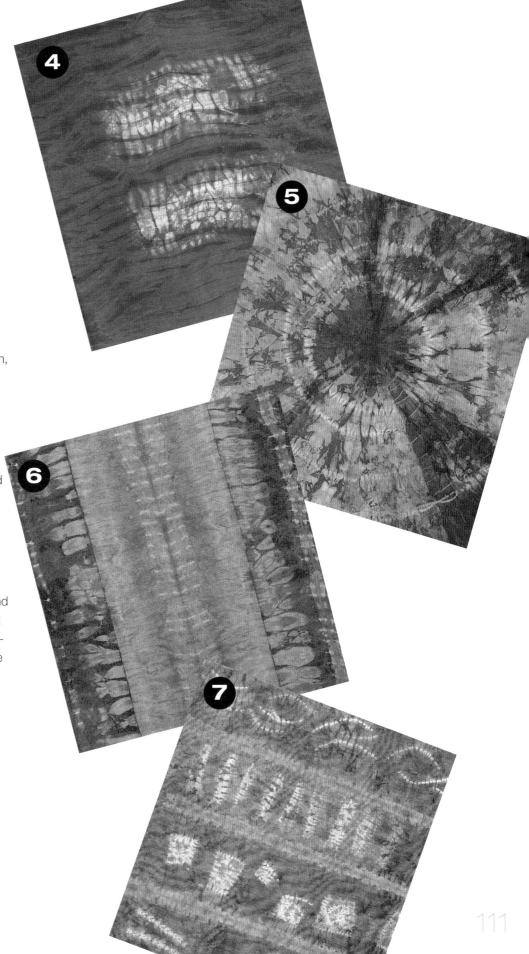

Finishing Techniques

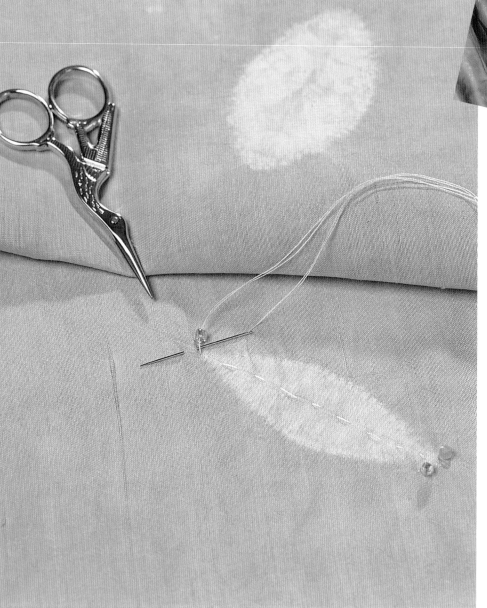

Arashi: silk organza and acid dyes

Shaping

Once you've pulled your shibori from the dye vat, rinsed it, hung it to dry, and untied it, you might wonder what's next. You have several options for how to finish it. One is just doing nothing. If you wait for the fabric to dry completely before you untie it, particularly when working with silk, then your shibori cloth will retain its shape, even after multiple hand washings. So, if you're interested in making a skirt with terrific pleats on the bias, resist the urge to untie it until the cloth is completely dry.

Heating the fabric during the dyeing process is a factor in getting it to retain its shape. When using acid dyes on silk, it's important to heat the dyes to just below the boiling point. This helps the silk retain its shape over time.

Sample 1

A piece of silk charmeuse was mokume-stitched on the bias and dyed with acid dyes.

Sample 2

This silk velvet was arashi-dyed with acid dyes.

Sample 3

Silk organza, marbles, rubber bands, and acid dyes were used in this swatch.

Sample 4

Create this texture with silk crêpe de chine, popcorn kernels, yarn, and acid dyes.

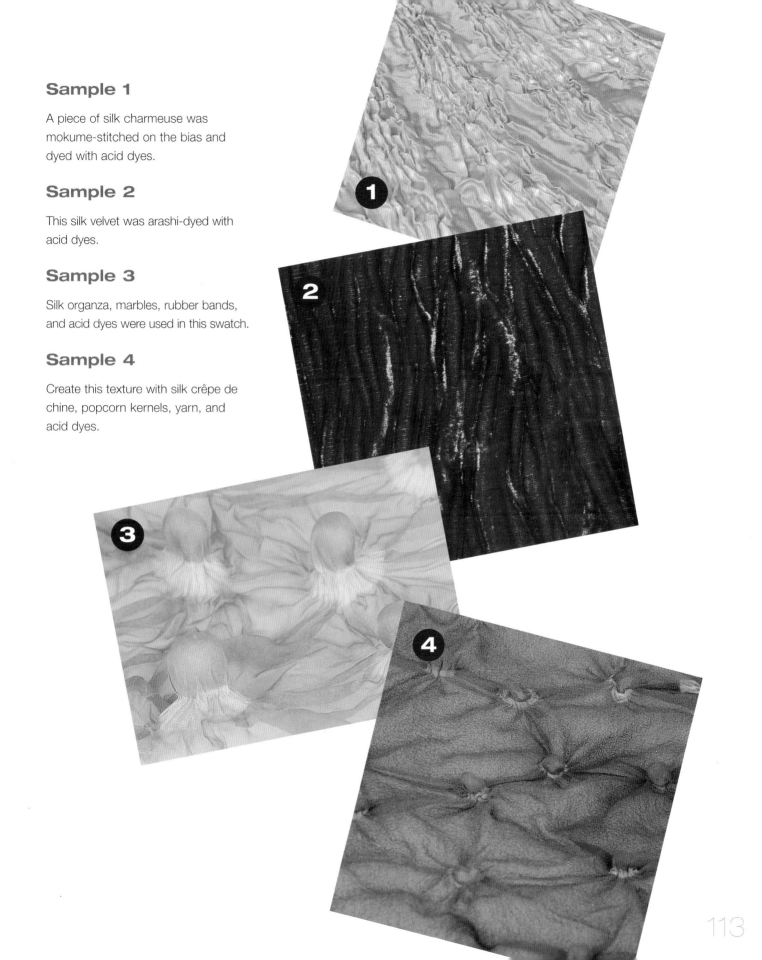

Another option for finishing your cloth is simply to untie and iron it before it is completely dry. By ironing the fabric flat, every change in pattern and color is featured.

A third way to finish shibori cloth is to iron and then embellish it. If you're interested in this finishing option, then you've got a whole world open to you. The following techniques are just the beginning. Check out the bibliography on page 127 to find more resources in creative embroidery, beading, printing, and painting on cloth.

Beading

The availability of beautiful beads is amazing. I find myself buying beads and storing them for some unknown project the same way I buy and stash fabric. I like to use a needle and thread to sew beads along lines in my shibori patterns to add extra depth. This works nicely on subtle pieces. And I find that bolder fabric calls for bolder beads. Be sure to affix the beads firmly to the fabric so they don't come undone during wear or multiple washings. A doubled quilting thread secured with strong knots works very well.

Sample 5

Here's silk charmeuse that was folded, stitched with running stitches, and dyed with acid dye. Small glass beads accent the resisted area.

Sample 6

This swatch was made with sueded rayon that was folded, machine stitched, and dyed with vat dye. The resisted area was highlighted with glass beads.

Sample 7

A silk charmeuse blouse was stitched and dyed with acid dye. Small glass beads were stitched on to emphasize the tiny marks made by the stitching.

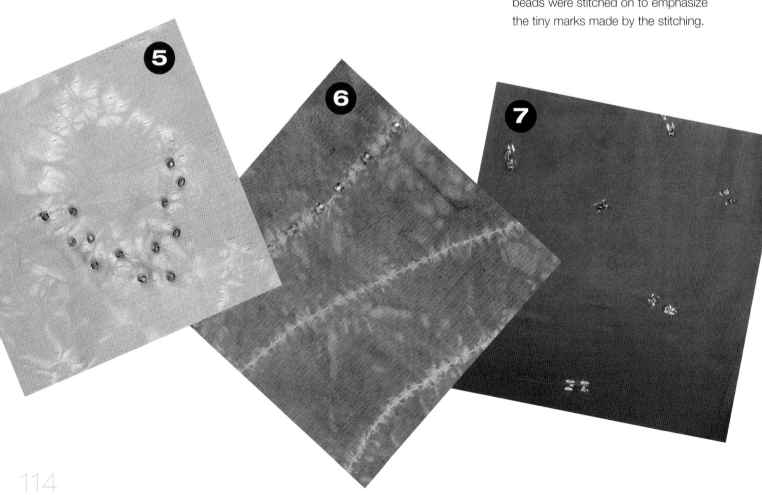

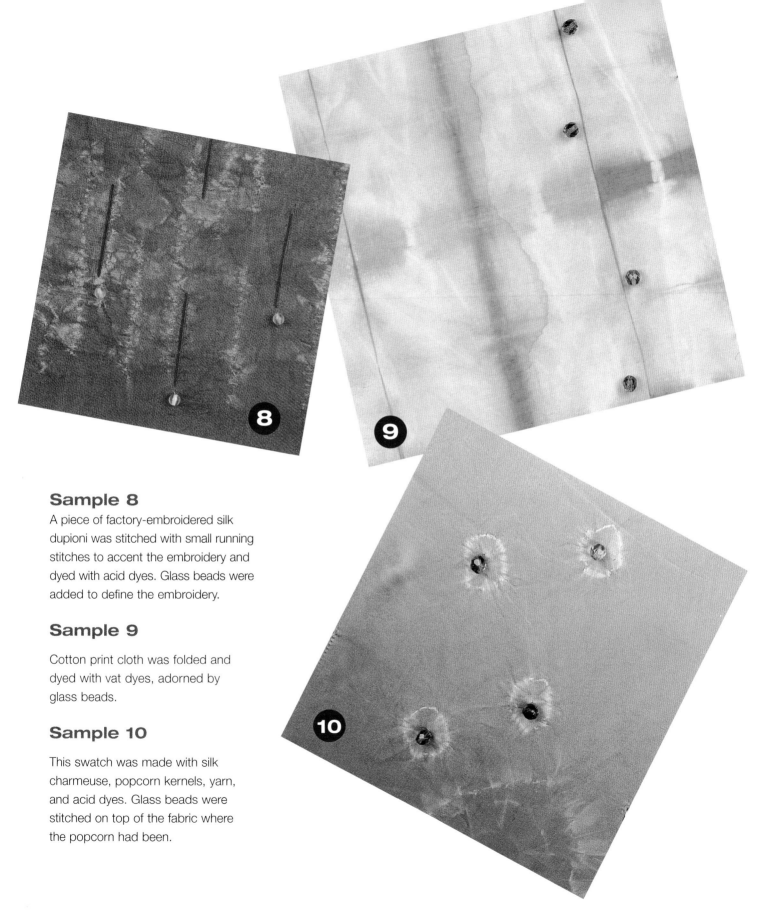

Sample 8

A piece of factory-embroidered silk dupioni was stitched with small running stitches to accent the embroidery and dyed with acid dyes. Glass beads were added to define the embroidery.

Sample 9

Cotton print cloth was folded and dyed with vat dyes, adorned by glass beads.

Sample 10

This swatch was made with silk charmeuse, popcorn kernels, yarn, and acid dyes. Glass beads were stitched on top of the fabric where the popcorn had been.

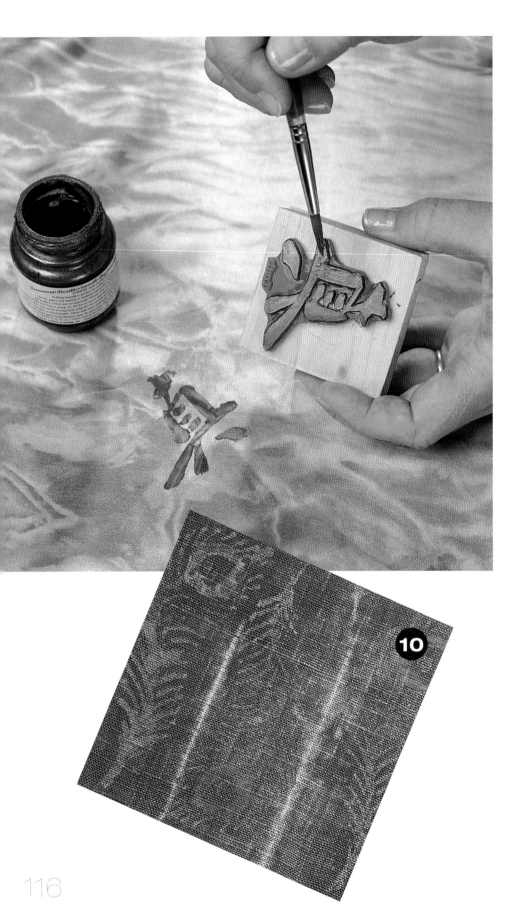

Stamping and Printing

Another process that can enhance shibori designs is stamping. Using precut stamps is a very easy process. All you need is the stamp, fiber paints, and a small paintbrush.

Before you stamp directly onto your cloth, do a test sample on a piece of cloth with the same texture as the cloth you'll be working with. It's easy to use too much paint the first time and too little the second time. The third time is usually a charm.

Spread a towel that has been folded once. Place the ironed cloth on top of the towel. Paint the stamp with the fabric paint, and then print. Make sure you use equal pressure on all areas of the stamp. Slowly peel the stamp from the surface of the cloth. Allow the paint to dry completely before ironing the fabric again.

Sample 10

This piece of linen was machine stitched, dyed with indigo, and stamped with a peacock stamp that had been painted with two different colors.

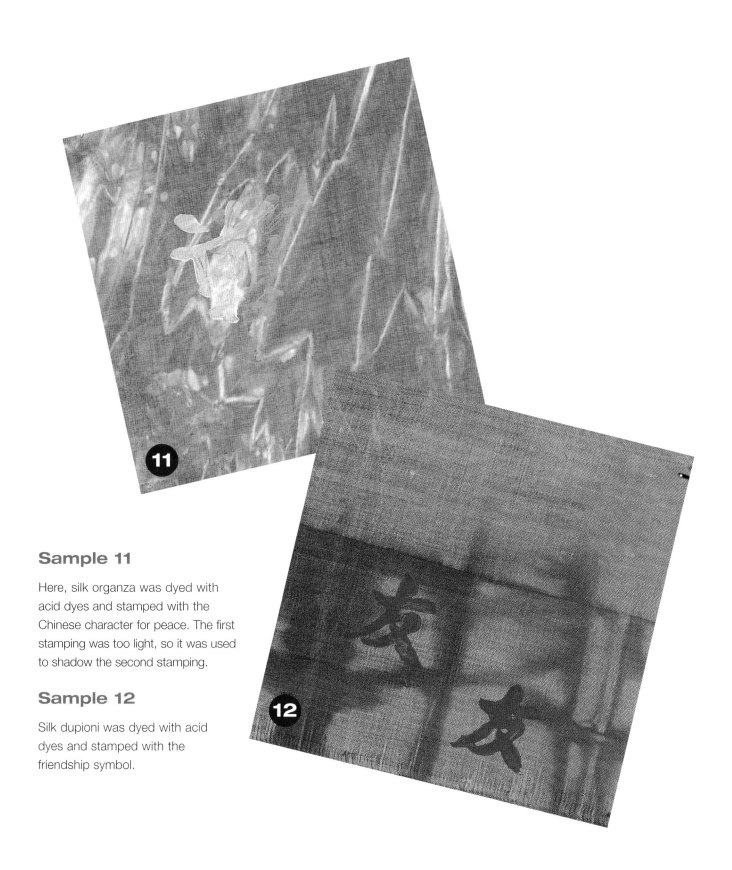

Sample 11

Here, silk organza was dyed with acid dyes and stamped with the Chinese character for peace. The first stamping was too light, so it was used to shadow the second stamping.

Sample 12

Silk dupioni was dyed with acid dyes and stamped with the friendship symbol.

Mono-printing is much like stamping, only you create the pattern on a flat piece of wood or other smooth object. Start by painting swirls or other images onto the wood, then slowly press the wood onto the fabric, transferring your image.

Sample 13

This swatch was made with cotton print cloth that was folded, dyed with vat dyes, and then monoprinted.

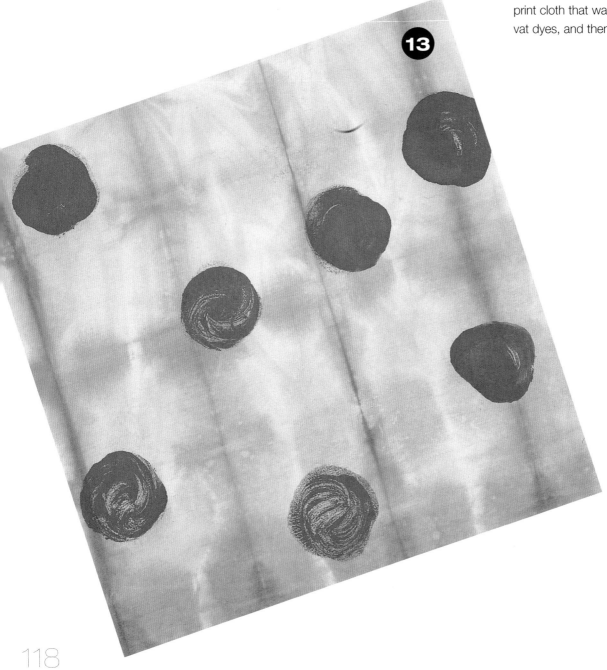

Photo transfer offers another way to print on fabric that has already been dyed. This technique works well when you've dyed a fabric that has large areas that resisted the dye or has subtly dyed areas that could use a little boost. You can transfer any image that can be copied with a color copy machine.

You can find photo transfer paper at most fabric stores. Before purchasing, just be sure to read the manufacturer's instructions so you know how to use it. I like to use images that I've created, either words that I've written or my own paintings. If you use your own work, then you won't have to worry about copyright issues. Take any copyright-free image that you would like to transfer and copy it onto photo transfer paper using a color copier. Then, simply place the photo transfer paper face down on your cloth and iron according to the package instructions.

The most readily available photo transfer paper is 8½ x 11 inches (21.6 x 28 cm). Unless you want that size to be transferred to your cloth, you can always cut the photo paper and arrange the images as you would like them on your fabric.

Sample 14

Silk dupioni was dyed with acid dye and embellished with photo transfer paper. The images shown on the fabric were created by copying a painting onto photo transfer paper, cutting the transfer paper into smaller squares, arranging the squares on the fabric, and ironing the images onto the fabric.

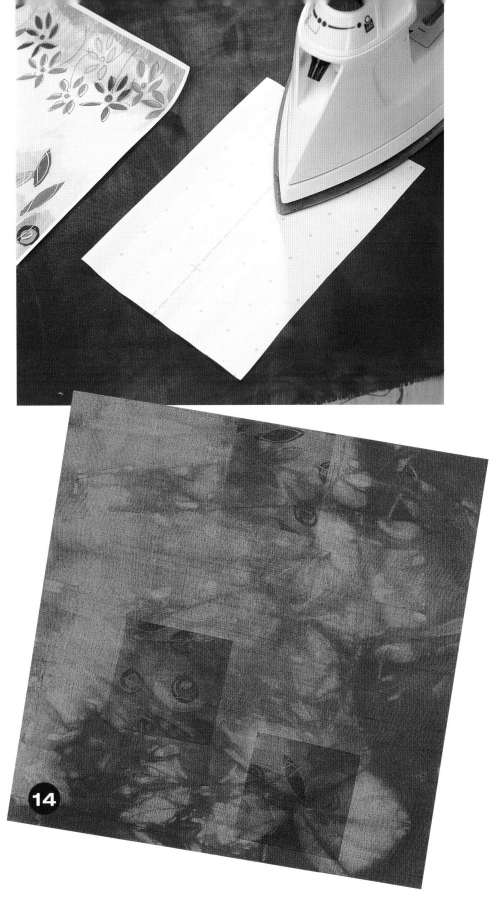

14

BLANKET STITCH

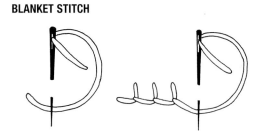

COUCHING

SATIN STITCH

FRENCH KNOT

CORAL STITCH

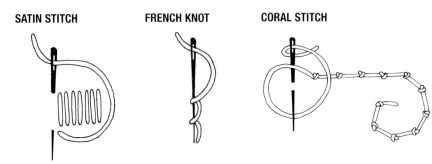

Embroidery

Embroidering shibori fabrics is another way of adding depth and pattern. I like to mimic a pattern that's already there to sharpen the flow of the design. The illustrations at the left are stitches that you can use to embellish your shibori cloth.

Sample 15

Here, silk charmeuse was folded, stitched with running stitch, pulled tightly, dyed with acid dyes, and embellished with embroidery along the dyed pattern. Cotton embroidery floss was used.

Sample 16

This swatch is silk dupioni that was arashi-dyed and embellished with embroidery to highlight the arashi pattern. Silk floss was used for this piece.

15

16

Another way to enhance the pattern is to draw directly onto the fabric with a pencil or permanent marker (depending on whether or not you will be able to hide the mark) and create a new pattern on top of the old one.

Sample 17

A piece of silk dupioni was arashi-dyed and embellished with designs drawn with a permanent marker. The designs were then embroidered using satin stitch and cotton embroidery floss.

For those interested in creating a subtle pattern, you may want to try embroidering with floss that's almost the same color as the fabric. This can be used to make a nice, quiet texture.

Sample 18

In this swatch, silk dupioni was arashi-dyed and embellished with embroidery using random satin stitch and silk embroidery floss.

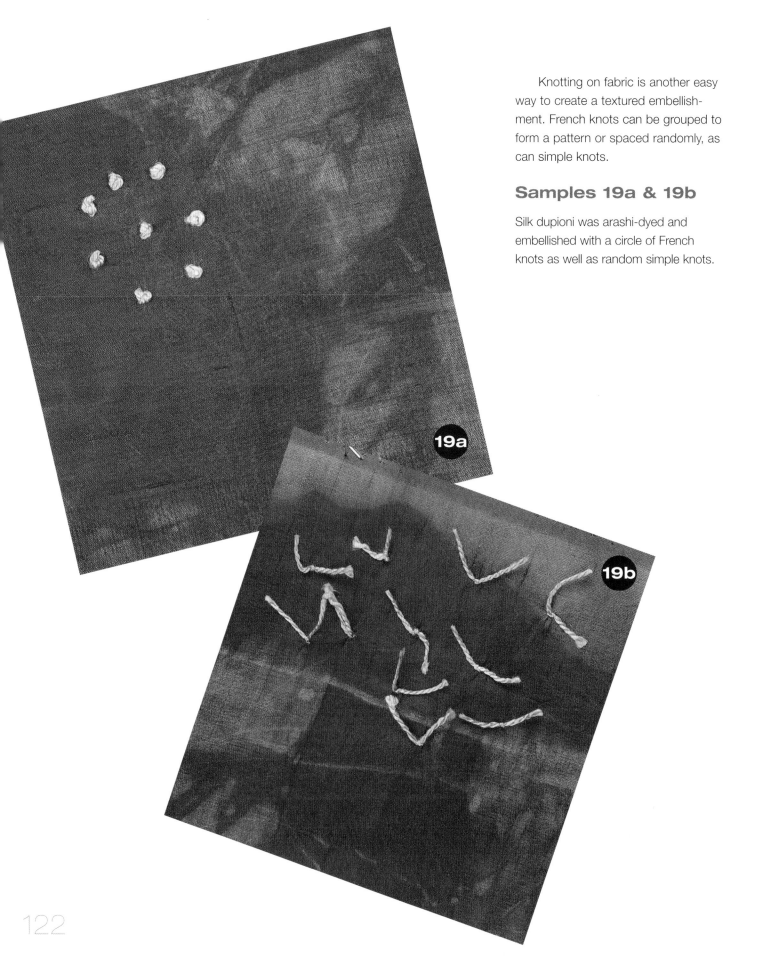

Knotting on fabric is another easy way to create a textured embellishment. French knots can be grouped to form a pattern or spaced randomly, as can simple knots.

Samples 19a & 19b

Silk dupioni was arashi-dyed and embellished with a circle of French knots as well as random simple knots.

19a

19b

Ribbon Accents

Ribbon is as fun to collect as beads and fabric swatches, so I have lots of it in my studio. I find that searching for the perfect accent to a piece of cloth can take hours and hours and still be fruitless, but often a ribbon I already have ferreted away is just the thing I need.

Sample 20

Here, sueded rayon was machine-stitched, vat dyed, and embellished by fusing embroidered ribbon to the fabric.

Sample 21

This factory-embroidered silk dupioni was folded, clamped with washers, dyed with acid dye, and embellished by fusing embroidered ribbon to the fabric.

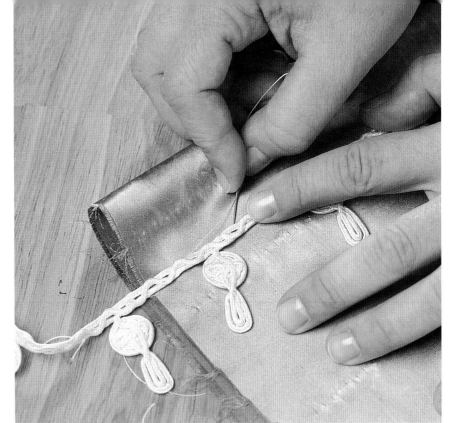

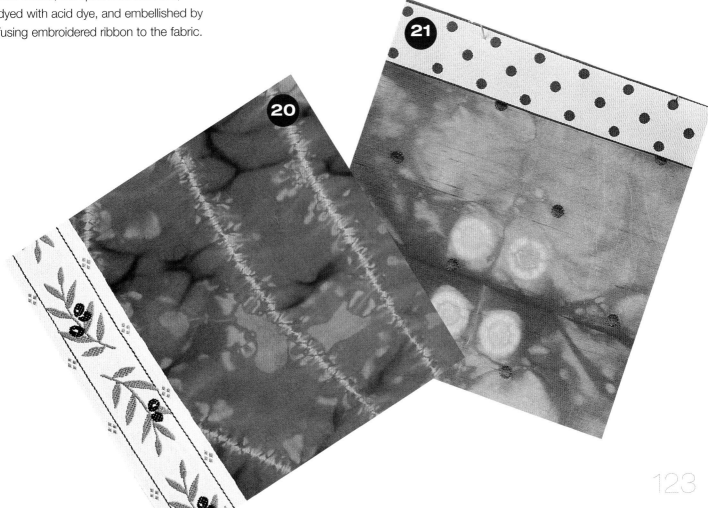

Miscellaneous Trim

You can add just about any type of trim to your shibori fabric, including tassles and feathers.

Sample 22

A shawl made of silk dupioni, this piece was created with the bound-resist technique. It was submerged in an acid dye bath and later embellished with feathers.

Templates

Enlarge to size.

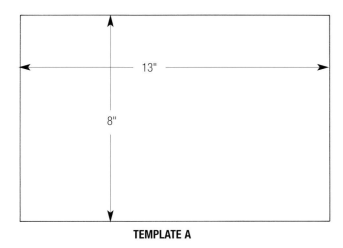

TEMPLATE A

13"

8"

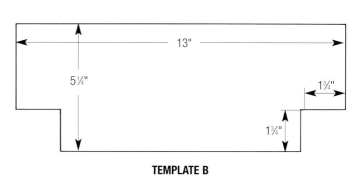

TEMPLATE B

13"

5¼"

1¾"

1¾"

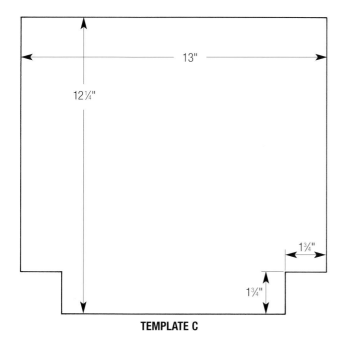

TEMPLATE C

13"

12¼"

1¾"

1¾"

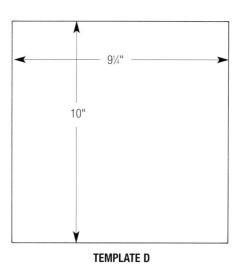

TEMPLATE D

9¼"

10"

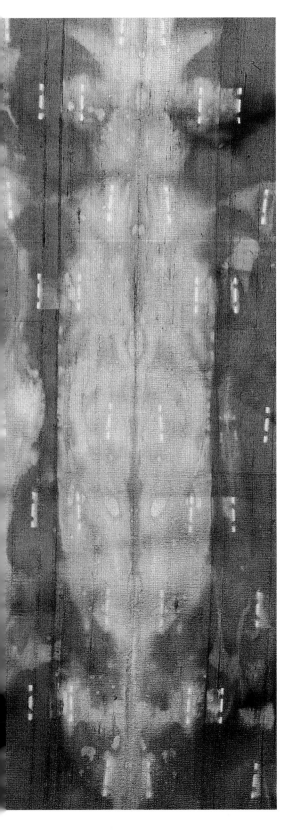

Acknowledgments

I would like to thank the artists and friends who have inspired me over the years and led me to work so fervently with dye and cloth. Deborah First, from the Savannah College of Art and Design, introduced me to the historic techniques of shibori and ikat. She passed her passion for tradition and history of cloth on to me, and I am very grateful to her. Without Yoshiko Wada's inspiration and research, this book might never have been written. My thanks go to the staff at Lark Books, especially Paige Gilchrist, Terry Taylor, Deborah Morgenthal, and Todd Kaderabek (for introducing me to everyone). Photographer Stewart O'Shields did a beautiful job photographing the images you see here. Stacey Budge is a terrific art director and I appreciate all of her hard work and sense of design. Valerie Shrader is one amazing editor; thank you for your organization, vision, kindness, patience, and friendship. My husband Malcolm, and children, Graham and Sarah, were always patient while I worked on the book and ready to play when I came down from the studio. Thank you to my family, who has always supported me in every-thing: my parents, Ron and Jo; my younger brother Bret; and my older brother Ron, who read the book with a kind and critical eye.

Contributing Designers

PEG GIGNOUX is a teaching artist based in Carrboro, North Carolina. Gignoux creates vibrant mixed-media works, art quilts, and handmade books for a variety of schools, museums and health care centers throughout North Carolina. Her clients include Duke Medical Center, Greensboro Hospice, University of North Carolina Hospitals, Hickory Museum of Art, Green Hill Center for North Carolina Art, and Elon University. Gignoux holds a B.A. from Kenyon College and a M.A. in industrial design in fibers from North Carolina State University.

REBECCA MANSKE is a stay-at-home mom in Asheville, North Carolina. After learning from her mother, Rebecca has been sewing seriously for three years and enjoys making handbags, children's clothes, and beginner quilts. She sells her handbags locally at craft shows and on consignment to support her fabric addiction.

Bibliography

Books

Bradford, Jenny. *Textured Embroidery.* Melbourne: Sally Milner Publishing Pty Ltd, 1993.

Brito, Karren K. *Shibori: Creating Color & Texture on Silk.* New York: Watson-Guptill Publications, 2002.

Dunnewold, Jane. *Complex Cloth: A Comprehensive Guide to Surface Design.* Bothell, WA: Fiber Studio Press, 1996.

Larsen, Jack Lenor, Alfred Buhler, Bronwen and Garrett Solyom. *The Dyer's Art: Ikat, Batik, Plangi.* New York: Van Nostrand Reinhold, 1976.

Proctor, Richard M. and Jennifer F. Lew. *Surface Design for Fabric.* Seattle and London: University of Washington Press, 1987.

Wada, Yoshiko Iwamoto. *Memory on Cloth.* Tokyo: Kodansha International Ltd, 2002.

Wada, Yoshiko, Mary Kellogg Rice, and Jane Barton. *Shibori: The Inventive Art of Japanese Shaped Resist Dyeing.* New York: Kodansha International Ltd, 1989.

Electronic Sources

Dharma Trading Co.
http://www.dharmatrading.com/

PRO Chemical & Dye
http://www.prochemical.com/

Index